The Power of Now

The Power of Now

How Winning Companies Sense and Respond to Change Using Real-Time Technology

Vivek Ranadivé

McGraw-Hill
New York • San Francisco • Washington, D.C. • Auckland • Bogotá
Caracas • Lisbon • London • Madrid • Mexico City • Milan
Montreal • New Delhi • San Juan • Singapore
Sydney • Tokyo • Toronto

McGraw-Hill

A Division of The McGraw·Hill Companies

5 6 7 8 9 0   QPF/QPF   0 4 3 2 1

ISBN 0-07-135684-3

The sponsoring editor for this book was Simon Yates and the production supervisor was Clare Stanley. It was set in Times by Multiscience Press, Inc.

Printed and bound by R. R. Donnelley and Sons Company.

McGraw-Hill books are available at special quantity discounts to use as premiums and sales promotions, or for use in corporate training programs. For more information, please write to the Director of Special Sales, McGraw-Hill, 11 West 19th Street, New York, NY 10011. Or contact your local bookstore.

CONTENTS

FOREWORD

The Power of Now: How Winning Companies Sense and Respond to Change Using Real-Time Technology is about the future. It is a book that details an emerging trend that will affect all of us, in one way or another, as we progress through the twenty-first century. It is a book about business, about speed, about competition, about technology, and about success in an increasingly global networked society.

I first met Vivek Ranadivé more than ten years ago, when he called to ask if he could borrow a workstation (he still hasn't given it back). At the time—the early 1980s—Sun was still a young company, even by Silicon Valley standards, and the Internet, UNIX, personal computers, even networks, were all relatively unknown technologies. The future was beyond our greatest expectations. Today, technology has become vital to the speed and performance of business. How the "event-driven" enterprise works—its technology, its culture and organization, and its business practices—is what Vivek describes in this book.

The systems Sun and TIBCO first installed together were for investment banks, which represent a sector of the financial industry that has the most demanding requirements of any industry I've encountered. All industries have mission-critical requirements, but the pace, pressure, and vast sums of money flowing through the systems of the world's largest investment banks and financial trading firms add a unique drama—and impact—to their technology requirements.

What we observed in that high-paced and high-stakes world has now begun infiltrating the halls of businesses everywhere— the extensive use of high-speed IP networks, powerful desktop computers, real-time information, and integrated information across many systems and sources are now increasingly the requirements of all businesses across all industries. Almost every significant business today is concerned about reducing the time it takes to accomplish a business transaction or bring a product to market. Processing customer orders in real time, over the Internet or over the telephone, and being able to tell your customers instantly the status of their orders, have become almost commonplace. Customers are demanding that everything be done faster—without sacrificing quality. They want what they want right away. At the same time, customers continue to demand more.

This obsession with speed and efficient business processes has only been further exaggerated by the emergence of the Internet. Technologies such as the Java platform and increasingly "intelligent" mobile devices—cell phones, pagers, set-top boxes, and even home appliances—are distributing computing power throughout all aspects of our lives. Sun's development of Jini is about extending Java to enable communications between all types of computing devices. With Jini, a laptop can plug into a network and immediately begin using "services," such as printers, on that network.

Functionality goes beyond mere plug-and-play and becomes "plug-and-work." But with all this connected computing power comes information. The Internet and the technology to integrate applications and computing devices will eventually mean complete information access and integration across the globe for business and personal use.

The new technologies that extend the reach and power of the computer and the network generate new possibilities for business. Those who can take advantage of these capabilities will benefit; those who can't will fail. It's really that simple.

Vivek's book is a great read. His topic is timely and is one that I believe will be extremely helpful for anyone trying to come to terms with how best to compete in this age of globalization, ubiquitous technology, and increasing competition. Being event-driven, you will find, involves more than simply employing technology to create real-time operations. Being event-driven means you have the tools, the mindset, and the organizational structure that enables you to do the right thing at the right time.

Scott McNealy
Chairman, President, and CEO
Sun Microsystems, Inc.
Palo Alto, California
July 1999

PREFACE

Over the years, I have been fortunate to interact with over 500 world-class companies that have taught me invaluable lessons. These experiences have provided me with the advantage of a unique perspective on how companies improve their competitiveness through technology. The challenges of the world taking shape around us today—the advent of the Internet, wireless technology, global markets, and the commoditization of everything—will require every company to constantly evolve its competitive edge.

The ideas presented in this book have their root in a technical concept I helped develop in the mid-1980s. The concept was to create a software technology that would facilitate the distribution of information across discrete software applications. The technology we developed allowed an exciting transformation in the way information could be distributed. Information was no longer a passive resource but rather an intelligent and active catalyst that could prompt meaningful business responses automatically and in real time throughout the enterprise.

This ability for information to trigger productive responses within organizations serves as the foundation for the central theme of this book—the event-driven company. Being event-driven is more than a technological characteristic—it is the infrastructure, culture, and mindset that I believe is required for companies to stay competitive today and in the future.

In writing this book, I took to heart a question often asked by a CEO friend of mine in response to overly theoretical business models: "That is all well and good, but what am I to do on Monday morning?" I have attempted to focus on the concept of the event-driven company by considering not only where we have been and where we hope to go, but also practical instructions on how to get there. It is my belief that the concept of the event-driven company has wide-ranging business implications. It is my hope that this book can stimulate new thinking, thus providing value to the readers who need to meet challenges that await them Monday morning.

Vivek Ranadivé
Palo Alto, California
July 1999

ACKNOWLEDGMENTS

Before I begin, I would like to thank the many individuals who have helped bring this book to fruition, especially the many colleagues and business partners who, over the years, have shared their technical skills and business insights that form the foundation of many of the ideas presented here. I am enormously indebted to my colleague Murray Rode, without whom this book would never have been realized. His intelligence and patience have been invaluable in transforming the thoughts of this book into a concept worthy of publication. George Turin, my friend and mentor, contributed greatly to this book. Suzi Berry's contribution and editing were greatly appreciated, as were Tiffany Gumfroy's research efforts. I'm also grateful to Bill Mandel for his help, and to Simon Yates, my editor, for his patience and support. I would also like to thank several colleagues who contributed to this book's content: Amlan Debnath, Jeff Harmon, Tommy Joseph, Rob Knourek, Raj Mashruwala, John Mathon, Fred Meyer, Dick O'Donnell, Jeff Risberg, Jayesh Shah, S. SriniVasan, Murat Sönmez, Alan Williams, and many others too numerous to mention. In addition, my business mentors, Steve Leavitt, Gerry Burnett, and Harvey Wagner, have impacted me greatly, providing important stimulation and inspiration for many of the ideas presented here. And, finally, I would like to dedicate this book to my three wonderful children and my wife, Deborah, who inspire me daily.

SELECT ENDORSEMENTS

"The Power of Now is about the future. It is a book that details an emerging trend that will affect all of us, in one way or another, as we progress through the 21st century. It is a book about business, about speed, about competition, about technology, and about success in an increasingly global networked society."

—Scott McNealy, CEO, Sun Microsystems
(from the Foreword)

"Vivek Ranadivé offers a fresh look at the hurdles businesses face in the new Internet Economy and why this will be a world where the fast beat the slow. Leading companies will use the power of the Internet to create and manage new world networks that will leave their competition far behind."

—John Chambers, President and CEO, Cisco Systems

"The Internet is the single-most revolutionary thing to happen to business since the invention of the computer. It's brought us closer together, while expanding the range of information and services we can access on a global basis. Everything is now a click-of-the-mouse away. Ranadivé's book provides an exciting look at how the Internet and information portals allow companies to profit from—and consumers to benefit from—the availability of real-time information and services."

—Tim Koogle, Chairman and CEO, Yahoo!

"A company that acquires, deploys, and wisely exploits real-time, active information is what Vivek Ranadivé dubs an "event-driven enterprise." Such companies sense and respond to the events that drive their business and achieve competitive advantage by creating virtual, integrated, real-time supply webs. Ranadivé provides an insightful look at how to stay ahead of the competition by staying close to customers."

—Dr. Eric Schmidt, CEO, Novell

"Any company whose value proposition relies upon the close collaboration of its business units and whose efficiency depends upon its ability to compress its supply chain needs more real-time intelligence in its IT environment. The virtual integrated real-time supply web advocated by Vivek

Ranadivé in this fresh look at business in the information age is a break-through. Ranadivé outlines why and how we must reformulate our business and IT strategies to compete in our increasingly global and networked society."

—Eric Benhamou, CEO, 3Com

"Ranadivé offers a captivating tale of the migration of technology from behind the closed doors of the information-intensive financial trading rooms of the mid-1980s to today's worlds of e-commerce, on-line brokerages, and multimedia communications. This book provides business leaders with important lessons on succeeding in today's information-rich environment."

—Peter Job, Chief Executive, Reuters Group PLC

"*The Power of Now* provides both the inspiration and blueprint for success in the Information Age. Ranadivé explains how information can be leveraged to gain competitive advantage by developing both the technical infrastructure to deliver integrated, real-time, active information and the human culture that transforms that information first into knowledge and then into informed, ongoing action."

—André Lussi, Chief Executive, Cedel Group

"Vivek Ranadivé's assertion that business must be strengthened with integrated, real-time, active information delivery systems to enable swift, creative responses across the enterprise is one that will likely become a key tenet of business strategy in the tweny-first century. This book will help you reshape your thinking about your company's IT strategy and how you think about business in general."

—Bill Pade, McKinsey & Company

"Ranadivé makes a strong case for the business imperative of becoming event-driven—that is, for turning your enterprise into an integrated organism that shares critical business information in real time on a global scale. *The Power of Now* offers the critical "how-to" recipe for obtaining bottom-line results in the twenty-first century."

—Larry Sonsini, Partner, Wilson Sonsini Goodrich & Rosati

THE EVENT-DRIVEN COMPANY

How many of these statements ring true for your company?

- Speed is God, time is the devil, and change is the sole constant.

- Business is no longer about return on investment but return on minutes.

- Yesterday's value-added products or services too quickly become today's commodities.

- Your customers expect customized products at commodity prices, immediately.

- Every time you look around, there are more competitors (or the old ones are gaining).

- Your people don't get the information they need, when they need it.

My guess is that most of these statements will ring true, because, as with all business people today, you're competing in the Information Age—a time, as Peter Drucker [1] warns, that "is far more competitive than any previous period in history, for the simple reason that with knowledge universally accessible, there are no excuses for nonperformance."

You may have already known that. What you may not know is what to do about it—what to do to raise your company above the ravages of creeping commoditization and gain that crucial, elusive *competitive advantage.* The current pace and global scope of business have accelerated everything, including the rate at which rust forms on yesterday's most profitable ideas, reducing high-margin products and services into low-margin commonplaces available from any number of sources.

I have helped more than 500 companies in many different industries stay ahead of deadly rust. My experience shows that the best way to outrun commoditization, maximize your company's return on minutes, and gain the competitive upper hand is to strengthen your business with integrated, real-time, active information delivery systems that report on significant business events throughout your entire scope of operation and enable swift, creative responses across the enterprise.

Coursing real-time, value-added information through every part of your organization is just the beginning. Information is nothing more than what Thomas Stewart [2], in *Intellectual Capital: The New Wealth of Organizations*, calls "the raw materials of knowledge." The company with a competitive advantage develops both the *technical infrastructure* to deliver integrated, real-time, active information and the *human culture* that transforms information first into knowledge and then into informed, ongoing action.

A company that acquires, deploys, and wisely exploits real-time, active information is what I call an "event-driven" company—one that, on one hand, instantly senses and responds to the events that *drive* its business and, on the other hand, uses the power of information to *drive* the development of new products and services.

Event-driven companies achieve competitive advantage by creating virtual, integrated, real-time supply networks for and with their customers. (The old term for supply network is "supply chain," but, as we'll see, there's no place for fixed *chains* in the new, wide-open global economy.) "Virtual" means that all elements of the supply network need not exist within the event-driven company's walls. "Integrated" means that every system within the event-driven company, its customers and its allies, is linked and intercommunicating via the event-driven information technology infrastructure. "Real-time" means instantly, zero-lag, as we speak: the time frame in which your customer wants satisfaction. "Supply network," finally, means the sum of the other three elements combined appropriately to solve your customers' problems. No matter what your company makes or does, it cannot survive as a product company alone. It can only survive by using the virtual, integrated, real-time supply network to solve your customers' problems.

Event-driven companies can be described as follows:

- They define themselves as being, above all, customer-centric.
- They create superior value for their customers.
- They cater profitably and transparently to their emerging Web customer base.
- They keep their sales and marketing ahead of the competition.

- They put the best information management tools in their employees' hands.

- They operate manufacturing and product development at optimal levels.

- They implement true knowledge management programs to leverage their valuable intellectual capital wisely.

- They maintain flexibility to weather market complexity and chaos.

- They update workers, customers, and partners instantly with crucial business information and events.

- They benefit from what appear to be "lucky accidents," which are, in fact, the benefits of being better informed sooner.

By deploying information technology to create and exploit active information, the event-driven company meets the definition of the "superior competitor" laid out by Michael Porter [3] in his 1980 classic *Competitive Strategies: Techniques for Analyzing Industries and Competitors*, "[a company that] anticipates shifts in competitive forces and responds to them before rivals, thereby exploiting change," and by M. Mitchell Waldrop [4] as "adaptive, creative . . . actively turning whatever happens to its advantage, evolving for better survival in a changing environment."

Becoming event-driven—staying ahead of commoditization and above the rust—is one of the key strategic challenges facing modern corporate leadership. In these pages I will explain *why* your company should become event-driven to survive and prosper in the emerging global business network, and *how to go about it*. Not just the usual generalities and motivational platitudes, but *specifics* regarding the following facets of the event-driven company:

- Information technology infrastructure

- Preference for value-creating "star" employees over just team players

- Leadership, management, and motivational models

■ Policies and practices regarding customers, partners/ allies, and competitors

I'll challenge you with litmus tests to see how close to event-driven your company is today, suggest ways to implement the cultural changes required to become event-driven, and offer advice on smoothing the transition. And I'll share some stories of highly effective companies that have become event-driven and enjoyed enormous gains as a result.

The Event-Driven Revolution

Despite the central position of technology infrastructure in the event-driven company, this book is not for the technology expert only. It is for anyone who wants to win in that mercenary territory known as modern business. Although the most complete implementation of the event-driven architecture utilizes a real-time software integration infrastructure, any wise business leader can benefit from this winning approach, because being event-driven is also a state of mind: a keen, continuous scanning of the horizon to anticipate events that change the status quo, and then applying event-driven tools to either shape change to the company's advantage or surf the changes one can't control in order to be first to the beach.

The event-driven state of mind is by no means an invention of the digital age. Its existence long preceded the wheel. In commerce, the event-driven state of mind has been in evidence for thousands of years wherever traders competed in the marketplace and practiced the fine art of custom-tailored, knowledge-based personal service to a clientele small enough to be managed by one brain. Today's event-driven technical infrastructure merely enables the event-driven state of mind to be projected on a global scale in the automated processes of business organizations, allowing those organizations to share critical information as quickly and easily as if they, too, were being managed by one brain: the event-driven information architecture.

The event-driven architecture features a technology called "publish/subscribe," which allows information about business events to be distributed in real time across private and public networks (i.e., intranets and the Internet). This technology started on the financial trading floor, has moved into a wide variety of enterprises, and is poised to enhance the possibilities of the Internet. I'll go into greater detail later, but what you should know now is that "publish/subscribe" can instantly and automatically deliver to everyone in your company's environment the information each person needs to create maximum value for your customers.

In contrast to the passive, "query me" client/server technology used in most companies, the event-driven infrastructure is "active," even somewhat aggressive. Through the publish/subscribe delivery mechanism, event-driven information is directed to help your people solve customers' problems. The value of event-driven information, as I'll illustrate, is increased as it moves through the enterprise. Event-driven systems allow automated processes to handle surprisingly high-level tasks as routine events without human involvement and—importantly—prompt human beings to intervene when exceptional events demand it.

The event-driven company thus "manages by exception," directing the vast majority of the company's human attention to the small minority of out-of-the-ordinary business situations that present both the most risk and the greatest opportunity. The event-driven infrastructure transforms companies into fit and flexible modern business organisms that embody Arie de Geus's [5] maxim: sustainable competitive advantage comes from the ability to learn faster than one's competition.

The event-driven company is distinguished from one that is merely current or contemporary primarily by its information technology infrastructure. All differentiating characteristics of the event-driven company flow from its IT architecture. The event-driven company utilizes the publish/subscribe information-delivery paradigm, whereas the contemporary company makes do with request/reply, which, as of mid-1999, still dominates the information technology world. You've used request/reply for years to "pull" information from a Web site. Stock prices, for example. You're *still* using request/reply pull even if your Web browser offers a stock-price channel that purports to "push" real-time stock quotes to the desktop. Fake push channels poll an information source—say, a server on the Internet or on your company's intranet—on a variable schedule, from every few seconds to every few days, and report any change they find. There are two major problems with fake push channels:

1. Though presented as "fresh" information "pushed" to your desktop, the data are neither fresh nor pushed. The information is as stale as the last interval in the polling schedule, and it has not been pushed to your desktop, it has been pulled there.

2. The more fake push channels try to appear fresh by increasing the frequency of polling, the more they congest the network with unnecessary traffic to and from the information source.

With publish/subscribe, your computer does not send out for the stock price every so often. It never sends out for anything. Having earlier "subscribed" to all changes in stock prices (each change is an "event"), the computer receives truly instant updates continually, in real time, whenever stock prices change, and that change is "published" onto the network. Each event is published just once and delivered to all subscribers, drastically reducing network traffic and congestion.

Place your finger on a red-hot stove. If our nervous systems were request/reply, you'd learn the stove's temperature the next time your nerves polled the stovetop. Fortunately, our nervous systems are event-driven, and they report the stove's temperature *instantly*. Which nervous system do you want for your company?

Is Real Time Really Necessary?

In talking with thousands of CEOs, CIOs, CTOs, and CFOs over the past 20 years, I've learned there are those who question the necessity of providing real-time information in their businesses. Isn't "pretty quick" good enough? No, it is not good enough. Not any more.

Remember when mainframes returned computational results on a batch basis—say, once a day? Most information systems managers thought the once-a-day batch was good enough. Then minicomputers and PCs came along that could make those calculations and offer results almost instantly. How many batch-oriented, mainframe-only businesses (and the MIS folks that championed them) survived the introduction of online transaction processing?

Remember, as well, when competitive athletes (or noncompetitive athletes who were serious about fitness) trained by simply walking, running, and climbing stairs? Then exercise technology came along that offered instant and continuous feedback: target aerobic heart rate, hill contour, number of calories burned per hour, elapsed time, and so on. Competitive athletes started posting better results after using high-tech feedback systems, and serious fitness seekers optimized their workouts with the extra information the new machines made available. Once exposed to the feedback from electronic workout gear, most people find it hard to return to the old-fashioned methods. My experience with business leaders indicates they feel the same way: Once exposed to the benefits of real-time information, they find it hard to go back to "pretty quick" batch information delivery. Then, of course, there's the issue of competitive advantage. Someone in your competitive environment is going to grab the high ground of real-time information delivery. It might as well be you out front.

Peter Drucker has remarked that, in the Information Age, winning teams write the score *while* they perform. The event-driven company's core strategy is to maintain superior competitive flexibility by structuring itself for immediate response to events in its ecosphere, modifying its organization and operations in real time to give customers exactly what they want as close to *now* as possible. Planning becomes a dynamic, interactive, real-time process guided by long-term intent and executed in real time at the customer interface. The strategy of competitive flexibility extends to relations with other companies as well. At any given moment, the usual suppliers can be swapped for new ones in the name of customer value, and other companies can quickly change costume from ally to competitor and back again, depending on the needs of the situation (tested against the company's unchanging vision).

A company need not be in high technology or anything close to high technology to reap the benefits of becoming event-driven. About the same time that the concept of the event-driven company was being born, Tom Peters [6] reported on a firm that used a primitive forerunner of active information to elevate the ultimate commodity, rags, above the grip of commoditization. In *Thriving on Chaos: Handbook for a Management Revolution*, Peters tells the story of Milliken & Co.'s shop towel division—"'shop towel,'" says Peters, "is a euphemism for 'rag'"—which sells shop towels to industrial launderers, who, in turn, rent them to their actual end users: factories. Milliken linked its computer system to its customers' systems so industrial laundries could place and track orders, access marketing ideas, study market research, and determine the fastest and cheapest way to ship freight, all online. Through the provision of timely and useful information, Peters reported, "Milliken turned the humble shop towel into a high-value-added, greatly differentiated product."

Though there is, indeed, plenty in this book for those who cannot or will not implement the event-driven IT infrastructure, it would be wrong to downplay the importance to any organization of information technology as a key to survival in the years ahead.

Information systems are not an overlay to what your company is doing. They should be integral to your strategy. In fact, it may be very hard to implement any change in strategy without leading that change from the IT side. A management consultant who has helped manage many companies' reengineering efforts recently told me, "We went into BPR thinking it was 80 percent about changing the processes and 20 percent about the technology, but we learned that doing good BPR turns out to be 20 percent about the processes and 80 percent about the technology, because bringing in the right technology *enables* the change in processes. Without the technology, it's very hard to make the changes."

Even a marketing authority—hardly the sort, normally, to be interested in such things—agrees. In *Real Time: Preparing for the Age of the Never-Satisfied Customer,* Regis McKenna [7] argues that his prescription for success—exploiting real-time information in a manner nearly identical to that of the event-driven company—can be filled by the right IT infrastructure: "Companies best equipped for the twenty-first century will consider investment in real-time systems as essential to maintaining their competitive edge and keeping their customers. They will use information technology to respond to changing circumstances, and, even more important, [respond to] customer expectations within the smallest possible lapse of time."

The Global Networked Society

There is one overarching reason for you to think seriously, right now, about how you can evolve your company to event-driven. When the global network currently under 24-hour-a-day construction is finally completed and the world becomes one unified, totally interconnected "trading floor," electronic communication will become the dominant forum and delivery platform for business activity.

It's hard to predict the precise moment when the growing ubiquity of the global network and the cost/benefit of doing business on that network will reach critical mass, but the moment is inevitable and fast approaching. For the first time in the history of networks, data traffic has now surpassed voice traffic. Doing business on the Internet offers such irresistible time and cost savings that businesses will struggle to put as many goods and services online as possible. For example, the offline/online ratio of labor required for overnight shipping of an audio CD is 54:1. The offline/online ratio of cost for that transaction is 8:1, according to the research firm ActivMedia, which commented: "Benefits of this magnitude create a [force] in the economy that draws everything into it that is not firmly attached to the physical world" [8].

The numbers are startling. As of April 1998 [9], use of the Internet by Americans was doubling *once every 100 days*, according to a U.S. Commerce Department report. In 1994, 3 million people worldwide used the Internet. By the close of 1999, eMarketer predicts there will be 130 million active Internet users worldwide, and 350 million by 2003 [10]. It took radio 38 years and television 13 years to gain 50 million domestic users. The Internet matched that figure in less than four years.

These Internet users are not just site-surfers and chat-room habitués. The Commerce Department cited Fortune 100 enterprises that are revamping their core business models to make better use of the network. The 12 business units of General Motors, for example, planned to buy $5 billion a year in materials online by 2000. Forrester Research estimates that global Internet commerce could equal $3.2 trillion in 2003, "5 percent of sales in the global economy" [11].

We are all bombarded with advertising and news articles that tell us how important it is to become an e-corporation. Ask 10 people what it means to be an e-corporation, however, and you'll get 10 different answers, but every definition will probably include some notion of Internet-based connections to customers and business partners. But an e-corporation involves much more than just the Internet, if you really want to realize its full benefit. E-business and e-commerce are speeding up what already feels like a very fast way of doing business. If you want to know what the completely networked customer of the near future looks like, look at your kid at one with his or her computer. That's your next customer: computer savvy, impatient, short attention span, willing to try new things but wanting satisfaction now.

Business processing cycles are becoming increasingly shorter as companies move toward the twin dreams of near zero-cycle product customization and zero-lag "cash to cash" (the cycle time between cash cost outlay for production/development and cash received for products sold). This increased speed depends on the real-time integration of all electronic processes within a company's operation, whether the process involves the buying or selling of stock or fulfillment of a product order. A company that has integrated all such processes is an event-driven company.

With the emergence of the Internet as a pervasive, global network, companies believe that embracing the Internet will lead them to increased, or renewed, prosperity. The Internet definitely opens up new avenues for taking advantage of event-driven business practices, but it can't replace a robust and responsive IT infrastructure inside the corporation. Many managers have not yet realized that being a successful e-corporation means dealing both with your internal processes and systems as well as your external means of servicing customers and connecting to business partners.

The growth of mobile-device Internet access and wireless technology is beginning to erase geographical and temporal considerations and the differences between landline and wireless communication. (This is especially true in the developing world—locus of many exciting twenty-first century opportunities—because there is no legacy infrastructure for users to cling to and slow things down. Witness the mass adoption of cellular telephony in developing countries without legacy landlines.) Business can increasingly be done on the network anytime, anywhere.

Meanwhile, incredibly inexpensive "smart" sensors embedded in nearly everything—creating ubiquitous machine intelligence—are bringing the physical and digital worlds closer. As we move about the physical world, our homes, cars, appliances, and our very bodies themselves will generate digital "events" that will be capitalized upon only by those event-driven companies technologically equipped to track, analyze, invent, and create value from them in the form of superfinely customized products and services.

Corporations will increasingly take advantage of targeted methods for communicating with customers, employees, and partners. The portal is emerging as one of the most powerful technological concepts for achieving such targeted communications. Portals, particularly corporate portals (i.e., one constructed for individual businesses), may have a bigger impact on IT than enterprise resource planning (ERP) systems (the core systems of your business for finance, logistics, human resources, and so on). The reason portals get so much attention is not for what they mean for the Internet, but for what they mean for the corporation. The portal is a simple, easy-to-use way of integrating and presenting multiple information sources and services to your employees, customers, and business partners, and can produce a dramatic return on your IT investment. A good portal is like a Web site on steroids—it creates a customizable view for individual users, and it is dynamic, updating in real time as business services and content change. Portals represent the means by which businesses can extend themselves over the Internet (and over wireless networks) to truly deliver on the hype of the Internet and e-business.

Once critical mass in the global network is reached—which you could argue has already happened—the rate of acceleration toward an integrated, network-based, real-time economy will present a serious barrier to entry for firms that have not prepared in time. Nonelectronic forms of business will become a liability. The emerging generation of consumers doesn't just want high-touch—it wants high-access.

Though we seem to be drowning in information today, there will be orders of magnitude more information in play in the networked world, increasing the business necessity of systems that automate as many processes as possible and filter what is worth our attention from what is routine. These systems will require human intervention only in the most exceptional situations, and they will deliver crucial, value-added information about the entire commercial environment where and when it is needed. That, in a nutshell, is the mission of business integration technology and the value being event-driven can offer any company seeking a competitive advantage.

What I Believe

In building my business and in helping hundreds of other companies around the world become event-driven, I've remained loyal to four basic ideas that have worked for me and my customers. I acknowledge that these concepts—perhaps because I developed the words with which they are expressed nearly 20 years ago—may sound quaint and obvious in today's environment. But, as I hope to convince you in the chapters ahead, the values that underlie these strategies remain critical measures for success in the global networked society.

1. The first, and perhaps the most essential, is that business must reinvent the way it uses information. Instead of viewing information as a passive resource languishing in a database waiting to be sought out, or as a treasure to be jealously withheld by the "owner," business information should be an active value enzyme that's distributed in real time to those in an organization whose optimal functioning depends upon it. The more people within a company who receive that information from real-time distribution systems, the greater the number of workers empowered and equipped to contribute to the overall success of the organization.

    In today's global economy, real-time information is not too fast for any business: Real time is merely *on time*, and anything slower is late. Christopher Meyer [12], in *Relentless Growth: How Silicon Valley Strategies Can Work in Your Business,* argues: "In traditional organizations, information becomes currency that is hoarded at each succeeding level of hierarchy. [But] in an economy based on knowledge"—of which the event-driven company is a prime example—"those without information can't contribute responsibly. Those *with* information find themselves compelled to act."

The other three ideas to which I've long remained loyal manifest themselves as strategic advantages for companies that transform their information distribution systems from passive to active.

2. I've already noted that an event-driven organization maintains superior *competitive flexibility* in order to steady its equilibrium and thrive in an increasingly chaotic global economy. No one, I believe, would argue against the necessity of maintaining *competitive flexibility,* though executing it is trickier than the phrase implies.

Remaining sufficiently nimble to pounce on new opportunities requires constant effort.

3. Event-driven information allows a company to engage in *superfine market segmentation.* In today's economy, *superfine market segmentation* refers to focusing product/service invention to meet the needs of individual customers as opposed to generalized market segments. This is true whether the "individual" is a person or a company. Evolution in the art of information distribution systems allows the event-driven company to define and serve a new, superfine market of one individual or less than one (the many markets within one consumer), fulfilling the dream of true mass customization. Customer and provider are brought together one on one, in a dialog made possible by the real-time exchange of information. This returns the commercial process to its one-on-one roots, while projecting it on a global scale.

4. The event-driven company *embeds its core competencies* in customers, partners, and allies in its sphere of operation. Event-driven companies often know as much about their customers' businesses as the customers do themselves. The partnership that results allows the event-driven company to embed its core competencies in other companies *at the other companies' requests.* Not by locking itself in with tricks or traps, but by making the relationship so increasingly beneficial that customers, suppliers, and allies can't wait to get more entwined.

The reason I first developed the idea for a publish/subscribe computing architecture was to provide the information technology infrastructure—the nervous system, if you will—for transforming traditional organizations into event-driven companies, imbuing them with these four basic advantages and thereby dramatically improving their performance. The event-driven concept has proved valuable from the trading floor to the enterprise and now the Internet (through the use of portals). True information publish/subscribe, as we'll see, is far more than just another technology trend. While by no means a panacea, publish/subscribe is a powerful technological idea that enables companies to revel in and profit from today's business maelstrom. It is a key to shaping and managing change in a fluid environment. It is a new way of thinking about information, which gives rise to a new way of thinking about, and conducting, business.

Event-Driven: The Metamanagement Theory

"Great," you say. "Just what my bookshelf needs: *another* management theory." There is certainly no shortage of those. In their book *Management Redeemed: Debunking the Fads That Undermine Corporate Performance*, Lex Donaldson and Frederick Hilmer [13] explore the myriad widely adopted cure-alls that have been prescribed for what ails business in the past 30 years (TQM, BPR, JIT—so familiar we know them by their initials). Theorists are turning out new, and often contradictory, theories as fast as Silicon Valley turns out next versions of its products, which is to say faster than anyone can try Version 1 before Version 1.1 is knocking at the door.

Not only have there been plenty of great new ideas suggested to improve your business, but when people try to put theory into practice and make the change, they often fail. Overall, four out of five corporate change efforts in the United States fail, according to Douglas K. Smith [14]. (On the upside, this theory/failure cycle has doubled many authors' publishing opportunities. I'm trusting my readers' executive abilities to make *The Power of Now Again* or *Enabling the Event-Driven Enterprise Reconsidered* unnecessary.)

Becoming event-driven is not, in fact, another management theory. Nor is it a retreat from, or a shortcut around, some of the smartest business thinking of the past 20 years. It's an amplifier, a clarifier, an enabler. It is a tool to help you realize, somewhat more successfully than Smith's 20 percent win rates, the business changes that make the most sense in your environment.

Becoming event-driven will allow your company to benefit even more from "process reengineering," the drive toward "total quality management," "zero-lag cycle time," "one-to-one marketing," "listening to your customers," and even "management by walking around." Whichever you choose, becoming event-driven offers a road map, an engine, a *means* of strengthening the efficacy of those philosophies and making your company as competitive as it can possibly be.

How Bechtel Corporation Is Event-Driven

Here's the story of one enterprise that felt it was losing its advantage to more nimble competitors and fought back successfully by adopting the event-driven infrastructure.

Bechtel Corporation, nearly a century old, is the world's largest construction firm. It manages an average of 1,400 projects a year, from skyscrapers to oil refineries to airports to the "Chunnel" under the English Channel. Beginning in the 1980s, Korean and Japanese construction companies began eating into Bechtel's dominance on the basis of lower price and better focus on specialized vertical markets. Bechtel at first fought back on price by instituting appropriate measures of the time, but these alone, it turned out, were insufficient for Bechtel to reestablish a clear competitive advantage. Bechtel decided to become event-driven in order to create superior customer value by lowering costs and improving on-time completion of projects.

In our initial conversations, the Bechtel people gave me an example of how a missing $45 connector bracket could seriously impact a multimillion-dollar project. If someone somewhere in the design process had changed a bracket design but forgot to tell the right people, everything and everyone could show up on the construction site on the big day minus the correctly designed bracket. This could literally lead to a multimillion dollar loss in wait time, as everyone sits around until the correctly configured brackets arrive from some foreign country. This example serves to underscore the fact that, in the construction business, delay can be death.

Upon examining itself, Bechtel realized it had developed a company-wide de facto cellular structure—elements of the company, each with differing expertise, were dispersed around the world and had developed "multiple inputs and outputs" (alliances and partnerships)—without developing the necessary ability, prescribed by Raymond Miles [15], "to interact with other cells to produce a more potent and competent business mechanism."

The solution Bechtel chose was to keep pockets of expertise wherever they made sense—for example, civil engineers in China, project managers in the United Kingdom, construction foremen onsite in India, computer-aided designers in the United States, human resources specialists in Germany—while constructing an event-driven IT infrastructure that not only linked the "cells" of the company into a virtual team but linked each person's function relationally to every other function. Everyone on a project shares the same bird's-eye view as it unfolds. When the smallest change is made to a design, news of that change is distributed in real time to the desktop of everyone who has a business interest in knowing about that change. If an architect moves a wall, electrical designers find out about it instantly and are prompted to change the wiring layouts; procurement people are alerted to order more drywall; and so on. These alerts are customizable and their routing and arrival are quite complex. The system is not omniscient. It must be told, through a system of programmable rule bases, which events should be flagged to which individuals. The method of flagging itself can be customized, taking the form of a scrolling banner, an e-mail, or a prompt window.

Organizationally, all company processes and workflows, worldwide, have been converted from sequential to parallel, meaning that information does not travel along a chain, stopping at each link—which in the past could take weeks—but arrives instantly, everywhere it is needed. Everything known about a project on site and everything known about it at the various hub offices are shared continuously, in real time. The event-driven infrastructure makes it impossible for anyone to be left out of the information loop.

The Age of Punctuated Equilibrium

Maybe the reason so many thinkers are turning out so many theories and selling so many books is that today's business leaders are more confused by the environment than ever before (it's hard to imagine Andrew Carnegie with a bookcase groaning under new management theories). Economist Lester Thurow [16] describes our interesting period in capitalist history as "punctuated equilibrium," by which he means, I think, that acting punch-drunk is a business leader's quite rational reaction to the current pace of change. The idea is amplified by Paul Ormerod [17], an expert on complexity theory at the London School of Economics, who describes the present as a time of essentially bounded instability where entities move between equilibrium and complete randomness.

"Complexity" is an important part of this book, and it is one to which I'll return often, because I believe business is now entering a period in which management theories that promote competitive flexibility by addressing complexity and its near-relation, chaos, will emerge as the only plausible scenarios in an increasingly implausible world.

Those of us in business are confronted by two apparently conflicting trends that seem to be accelerating in opposite directions. On one hand, our focus is expanding as we do business on a global scale and throw wide our companies' nets to girdle the world. On the other hand, our focus is narrowing as we develop evermore sophisticated, one-to-one micromarketing techniques to enrich and extend the relationship with individual customers (people or businesses).

Business leaders are being asked to look through a telescope with one eye and a microscope with the other. The resulting view, not surprisingly, is complex and chaotic. The same effect is at work in our sense of collapsing time, as the future rushes insistently toward us: I used to half-jokingly tell people that "one day" Bayer A. G. would sell me "Vivek's Bayer Aspirin," specially formulated for my personal habits—a bit of caffeine added for headaches on business mornings, a bit of St. Johnswort for headaches on weekends. One day is almost here.

Many Internet portals use sophisticated ad "servers" to display banner ads targeted to an individual's preferences as determined from a database of past buying practices. When prophecies are fulfilled as quickly as they are uttered, chaos and complexity reign.

It is in this boiling sea of change that a company must, however reluctantly, seek its bounty: "human organizations must operate in chaos," says Hertford Business School's Ralph Stacey [18], "if they are to be continually creative." In this period of punctuated equilibrium, the event-driven infrastructure offers an opportunity for your company to surf the chaos to your company's advantage.

Event-driven managers understand the significant implications of living on the windowsill. First to go is the comfort of long-range planning in the traditional sense. As David Hancock [19], CEO of Hitachi PC, puts it, "Today, plans are obsolete the minute they're written. The best you can do is pick a hilltop, point everyone there, and start fighting." When Lou Gerstner first took over at then-beleaguered IBM, he startled people by answering a question on his strategy for IBM by saying that IBM didn't need a strategy, it needed excellent customer-centric execution.

Another comfort lost in today's global economy is the tendency to bear down managerially on safe, familiar, results-producing routines instead of tackling the tougher challenges. This won't happen with the event-driven infrastructure, which handles routine tasks automatically and calls for human involvement only with problems no automated system can handle—what's called "management by exception." Putting the majority of your effort into the minority of tasks that hold the most promise and the most risk is threatening to those who crave the comforts of the familiar, but it is the only way to have a chance of shaking the rust and leading the competition.

For the event-driven company, times of chaos and complexity are times of great opportunity. Instant, targeted, interactive information provides the unique equilibrium that allows the event-driven company to walk the knife-edge separating fluid and innovative adaptability from anarchy. I believe that many companies today underestimate the power of information technology to enable positive change in business processes.

If this description of barely controlled but beneficial evolution sounds vaguely familiar, it should. The Internet has danced along this particular knife-edge from its inception. Becoming event-driven offers companies the opportunity to emulate the best of the Internet's philosophical experience by evolving into *competitively flexible* structures that continually self-organize and reorganize around a single goal.

Join the Economy of Increasing Returns

The highest goal around which an event-driven company can self-organize is to create superior value for customers, thereby increasing its own value. I would argue that making the financial and human investment in becoming event-driven dramatically increases a company's value, not only in terms of bottom-line performance but by redefining a company's position in the business universe. Santa Fe Institute economist Brian Arthur [20], a leading thinker on complexity, divides business investment into two categories: those of "diminishing returns" and "increasing returns." "Diminishing returns hold sway in the traditional part of the economy—the processing industries," whereas "increasing returns" are enjoyed by businesses devoted to "processing information" and are adept at reading the trends of their marketplace and jumping on opportunity. The event-driven infrastructure is designed to maximize your ability to do just that by making information more available. This is a simple but powerful idea in a global networked economy where success is increasingly defined as operating in real time. Thus, a company that makes the investment in becoming event-driven rises into the economy of "increasing returns"—unlike physical resources, event-driven, active information does not wear out; it becomes more valuable the more it is used.

Converting your organization to event-driven, therefore, is a bit like converting an energy plant from fission to fusion. The more widely information assets are circulated and recycled through the event-driven company, the more powerful and valuable they become.

This Is Not a Silicon Valley Book of the Nineties

A word of reassurance: I am not about to give you a familiar Silicon Valley–style lecture about eliminating executive parking spots, putting the CEO in the same kind of cubicle as everyone else, burning neckties, and serving the workforce free donuts or bagels on Friday mornings. If you want to do any or all of these things, please don't let me stop you, but in my mind they have absolutely nothing to do with inspiring your workers to create more value for your customers and/or develop loyalty to your company. Only two things are going to do that: providing your employees avenues to advance themselves continuously by increasing their value in the business world, and rewarding them not so much for coming to work as for making exceptional efforts on behalf of your customers. At my company, my goal isn't to provide employees lifetime employment but lifetime *employability.* There are handsome bonuses for those who excel, but no free donuts.

It All Starts with the Customer

Very much like the mantra "be close to your customer," "creating customer value" is such a familiar, timeworn phrase that it barely registers . . . even though it is one of the few existing differentiators that can create competitive advantage! The classic differentiators outlined by Michael Porter and others—cost leadership, quality, focus, speed—have themselves become commodities. They are now simply the ante to sit at the table—the price of market entry. Customer value is the only weapon with which business can hold creeping commoditization at bay. It's interesting that the most modern technology is now being harnessed to recreate the most old-fashioned commercial virtue—knowing your customer—as the latest in business defense strategies.

Don Peppers and Martha Rogers [21] observe that one-to-one marketing, like becoming an event-driven company, "wasn't feasible just ten years ago—although it's a direct reflection of how business was practiced 110 years ago! Technology has brought us back to an old-fashioned way of doing business." We all live in Marshall McLuhan's Global Village now, and we're using technology to go "forward to the past," harnessing machines to "know" each customer in our "village" as personally as small-town corner merchants once knew their clientele. Corner merchants had no computers, but they did business in an event-driven state of mind.

Customer-centricity—starting with the customer and solving the customer's problems—is the mother of all good business practices. I have been customer-driven from the age of 25, when I had a great idea for a product and wanted to build a prototype before looking for a customer. I was persuaded by wiser heads that problem solving for customers ought to drive innovation and implementation, not the other way around. I learned that letting customer needs inspire product invention allowed me to partner with my customers and assume part of my customers' risks as I developed solutions, thus embedding myself in the customers' processes. As things turned out, my mentors were correct, and my first customer helped enormously in shaping my first product (as other customers have with every product and service since). His name is Robert Rubin, and, as you probably know, he went on to become secretary of the treasury.

My experience with Rubin's Goldman Sachs, which I'll detail shortly, moved me from being a firm believer in the "design, build, sell" model, in which the product comes first and then goes looking for a problem to solve, to accepting the value of the "sell, design, build" model, which creates products that are literally customer solutions. As I learned, there is always time later to "productize" solutions that promise to deliver value to customers in related fields. (Likewise, I learned the "trick" of near-customization: Crafting custom solutions from stock parts or services allows one to solve a customer's problems one to one while keeping your own costs at off-the-shelf levels.)

To underscore the primacy of solutions over products, I often repeat to my employees the old maxim: Drill-bit manufacturers should never forget that their customers don't value a drill bit; they value a hole in the ground.

The Value of Value

I'm often surprised by how many business executives confuse *value* with *profit*. They are not the same thing. In the event-driven company, profit is a *consequence* of creating value. Profit is what piles up while you're busy solving your customers' problems. The value of the event-driven information system, of course, is that it brings you, your customers, and all those operating in your sphere together in real time, without barriers of distance or technology incompatibility, to collaborate on solving each other's problems. The wonderful by-product is profit.

Let's Get Busy

Regardless of what *your* company makes or does, it needs timely, integrated, value-added, active information about customers, markets, potential suppliers, and competitors circulating through its entire structure to stay ahead of the pursuing specters of poor return on minutes, rising rust, and increasing commoditization. But becoming event-driven will not be easy. It will transform your company—not only in such functional processes as marketing, sales, planning, compensation, human resources, and manufacturing, but in its basic organization and culture. As with any change, there will be those within your company who will feel threatened and resist. It's human nature to fear change. As the leader, you are the one responsible for explaining strategically why the change must come and how it will benefit everyone who does business in or with your company. Then you must set an example, by your behavior, of how to embrace and benefit from the changes you have set in motion.

In the following chapters, I will deal in greater depth with many of the themes sketched out in this one. Some of the business and management philosophies I'll discuss may be familiar to you. On the other hand, you may find other familiar concepts of "new business thinking" missing entirely, for a simple reason: I don't want to waste your time telling you things you already know. In writing this book, I'm assuming that business leaders ready to enter the new ecosystem of the event-driven company have already implemented, or at least thought through, the popular reinvention nostrums of the 1980s and 1990s and are ready for something that amplifies the best of recent business thinking and discards what doesn't work. That's why I will continually distinguish between the "contemporary" company, which is fast becoming yesterday's news, and the event-driven e-corporation of the twenty-first century.

Nor do I want to waste time preaching to the choir. I hope we all agree, for example, that downsizing isn't a realistic business strategy but simply a great technique for making your business disappear. And that some of the classic differentiators outlined by Michael Porter are no longer differentiators at all but simply tickets to the dance—quality, for instance, is no longer a competitive advantage, it's merely the assumed price of entry to the marketplace.

By the time a company is ready to become event-driven, it's not unreasonable to surmise that the organization has already done what's been prescribed during the last two decades—flattened its departmental silos and stovepipes, created cross-functional teams around specific projects and goals, instituted collaboration with "upstream" and "downstream" players, mastered market segmentation, and so on. Likewise, the company's processes, I expect, have long ago been reengineered along Michael Hammer's [22] suggested lines: minimizing non-value-added work by replacing sequential processes with integrated, holistic processes that achieve results. In his book, for instance, Hammer uses the example of GTE customer service, which created the position of "customer care advocate," equipped to gather information from customers with troubled phone lines; check the lines for actual malfunctions; and dispatch repair people, a sequence that formerly required time-consuming cross-communication among three people working in three separate stovepipe departments.

This book is written to take business leaders from the now-outdated contemporary company to the new frontier of the event-driven company without tarrying to repeat what you already know. Why waste time and kill trees?

There Are No Silver Bullets

I will, obviously, be saying quite a bit in support of becoming event-driven. And yet, becoming event-driven is no magical silver bullet. It will not cure inadequate processes. It won't turn poor enterprise applications into effective ones. If your organization lacks content, becoming event-driven will not provide it. It will not turn a bad company into a good one. In fact, the finer your existing processes, the stronger your installed applications, the more content your company already generates, the more becoming event-driven will help you deploy those assets in intelligent, organized ways to achieve a competitive advantage.

Having said that, I must admit the hard truth: There is no *permanent* competitive advantage in today's business world. Nevertheless, one can arm a company to fight for that advantage, and the best way to do that, in my view, is to blend information about all apropos events–events that occur inside and outside the company–into a constant flow of integrated, real-time, value-added information that circulates throughout the entire ecosystem in which your company does business. Becoming event-driven will certainly not guarantee a competitive advantage, but it will guarantee that you will be better equipped for the fight.

CHAPTER **2**

BECOMING EVENT-DRIVEN

Is Yours an Event-Driven Company?

Ready for a surprise? Take this litmus test:

- Do you form long-term alliances with partners and suppliers?
- Do you belong to an industry *keiretsu*?
- Is your company's operational focus on quality?
- Is your corporate culture egalitarian and consensus-oriented?
- Do you prefer to hire team players?
- Do managers fully empower workers?
- Do you have a formal strategic planning process to map out your business over the next several years?
- Do you focus on your competition and adjust your strategy accordingly?
- Are the customers your CEO deals with mostly happy customers?
- Do you have a client/server information technology system that emphasizes database technology?

If you answered "yes" to any of these questions, yours is *not* an event-driven company. Contemporary, perhaps, but not event-driven. This may come as a disappointment to leaders who pride themselves on their flat organizations and egalitarian corporate cultures staffed with team players. Those were fine for the late twentieth century. Displaying such characteristics—and the others listed above—does prove that one's company has evolved beyond the dinosaurs. But today a new century looms. Here's how the event-driven company differs from the merely contemporary:

- The event-driven company does not form alliances. It eschews the cozy comforts of the *keiretsu*, with its interlocking relationships, because a *keiretsu* is a closed environment. Value thrives best in open systems. The event-driven company is part of an information-intensive cellular structure, the virtual, integrated, real-time supply web. Its relationships with suppliers and partners/allies change quickly, and unapologetically, when convenient. (And the company is prepared for the same treatment in return; in fact, it welcomes the same treatment as a way to prove its continuing value.)

■ Its operational focus *assumes* quality, automates basic processes to achieve quality, and takes the next step to "management by exception."

■ Its culture is not consensus-oriented. It is meritocratic and fiercely entrepreneurial (at all levels).

■ Team players are OK. But the event-driven company prefers to hire—and tolerate the quirks of—"star" employees, who are often prima donnas. Star employees are quick to pursue emerging trends and take the risks that bring the highest rewards.

■ Leaders don't empower workers; they organize the company's structure so that workers *empower themselves*.

■ The event-driven company's planning horizon is one year or less. Anything longer is astrology. At the same time, as we'll see, the event-driven company is organized around long-term *intent* with an eye more on tomorrow's revenues than today's.

■ There's no need to watch the competition if you're spending enough time watching and learning from your customers. The competition can be a fatal distraction: Look at what happened to Novell when it became obsessed with Microsoft. Perfectly profitable companies went down the tubes trying to best competitors that didn't have to be defeated.

■ Meeting with happy customers may make for an excellent day on the golf course, but it teaches little. A key job element of the event-driven CEO is talking face to face with *unhappy* customers to find out why they're unhappy and what can be done to change that situation.

■ Client/server database technology is a passive, request/reply paradigm that alone fails to recognize the vital business power inherent in active information. The event-driven company's information technology infrastructure integrates all applications, databases, and information-producing sources in the company's sphere and distributes real-time, value-added information where and when it is needed.

Your Company Needs to Change, but How?

You wouldn't be reading this book if change weren't on your mind. The business world is shape-shifting so rapidly that stasis is a death sentence. Creating a fresh and sustainable competitive advantage for your company is mandatory. The question is how much and what kind of change does your company really need to gain that advantage.

Is becoming an event-driven e-corporation the right change for you to make? I believe that becoming event-driven is the most powerful means to achieving a sustainable competitive advantage in today's global business ecosystem, but before you choose the event-driven route you must be certain that becoming event-driven is a battle you're ready to fight . . . *and win*. Because becoming event-driven is not for everyone. The benefits are universally appealing once the destination is reached, but the road is a tough and demanding one. You must be willing to shake up the way you do business and be willing, as well, to lead your employees in coping with, embracing, and extracting the most from changes that may, at first, strike them as radical and demanding.

Moreover, as Regis McKenna [23] says in *Real Time: Preparing for the Age of the Never-Satisfied Customer,* when it comes to "the technologies of real time," of which the event-driven infrastructure is a premier example, there's only one way to learn what's really involved: "by adopting them and putting them to practical use." You've got to jump in, make the big investments of blood, sweat, tears, and money, and do it. The benefits? Describing the real-time/event-driven company, McKenna continues: "[companies] will deploy [the technologies] not to predict the future but to live virtually on top of changing patterns and trends affecting every sphere of their business environment, making rapid and continuous refinements in their way of doing business."

That sounds good. Everyone wants to do that. But is becoming event-driven really the right way for you to get there? One way to tell is to read the comparisons between the contemporary and event-driven companies illustrated in Table 2.1 and decide on which set of structural assumptions you'd prefer to embark in the next five years.

As I mentioned in enumerating the differences between the contemporary and event-driven companies, the event-driven company's planning horizon is very near-term, less than a year, but its view of the future or "intent" is medium- to long-term. An event-driven company initially reacts in "short cycle time" to flock resources around the invention, production, and delivery of a product or service to solve a customer's need. The compounded knowledge and expertise generated by multiple short-cycle invention processes is then circulated, refined, and shared with the organization to create expanding, sustained-growth value on a very long cycle.

This is the correct strategy for any company that is customer-centered. You must join your customer in anticipating his or her needs a few years out, while maintaining the mutual flexibility to change as immediate developments suggest. It is much wiser to aspire to the significantly higher margins earned by serving the same customers over a period of time than by constantly identifying, qualifying, and landing new customers. The event-driven company, therefore, has its eye more on tomorrow's value than today's revenue.

It's interesting to note that even investors, a group often characterized as myopically obsessed with the next quarter's earnings report, often place greater value on companies looking toward tomorrow's revenues even if today's are not significant. The actual annual revenues of Internet portal Yahoo!, for example, were approximately $203 million in 1998, but its market capitalization is $34 billion. Novell, which brought in $1 billion in 1998, is capitalized at $9.9 billion, while Amazon.com, who

TABLE 2.1

Characteristics
of an
Event-Driven
Company

Characteristic or Practice	Contemporary Company	Event-Driven Company
Business strategy	Long-term strategic plan guides actions	Medium-to long-term intent, but short-term planning horizon
Competitive posture	Study and understand your competition	Study and understand your customer
Management style	Consensus oriented management	Entrepreneurial leadership, star system
Operational focus	Continuous monitoring to achieve quality	Quality is assumed, focus is on exceptional trends and events
Corporate culture	Egalitarian	Meritocratic
Recruiting	Hire team players	Team players are good, but prima donnas bring the greatest value
Implicit company/ employee compact	Promise of lifetime employment	Opportunity for lifetime employability
Employee career management	Company manages your career	Employee manages own career
Information technology	Database-centric, passive, demand-driven	Information-centric, active, event-driven
Partnership model	Formal or informal keiretsu	Shifting alliances and "coop-etition"
Corporate anthem	Souza march	Jazz improvisation

had similar annual revenues, is worth far more: $20 billion. The best example may be IBM at $82 billion in revenue in 1998 with a $241 billion market capitalization versus Microsoft at $14.5 billion in revenue in 1998 with a market capitalization that is nearly double at $396 billion (as of July 1999). The market valuations of these companies are clearly not based on revenue alone, but on their potential impact on the marketplace. I believe it is the "virtual" footprint of these companies within the global networked society that drives their valuations.

In deciding if becoming event-driven is for you, it might help to consider the operational and strategic differences between a company focused more on today's revenues and one focused on tomorrow's. Christopher Meyer [24] outlines those differences in his book, which analyzes Silicon Valley's most successful companies for commonalties. Read down each column and see where you want to be:

Today's Revenues	*Tomorrow's Revenues*
Steps are predefined	Steps are undefined
Steps are mostly sequential	Steps frequently nonlinear
Functionally focused	Cross-functional work team
Redoing work costs money	Reworking is part of learning
One right way and result	Several right ways and results
Facts are clear	Facts are fuzzy
Easy to measure	Tough to measure
Forecasting helpful	Forecasting difficult
Short cycle time	Long cycle time [i.e., long-term intent]
Many common causes	Many special causes
Traditional players/roles	Involves new players/roles

To my mind, this chart defines the differences between a company heading for the rustpile and one that has a fighting chance to create and sustain competitive advantage. If you read the characteristics on the right and said to yourself, "Well, *of course.* That's the way modern business is: chaotic, fractured, confusing, unsettling; now tell me how to profit from it," then you will be, if not comfortable, at least not excessively disoriented as you drive toward becoming event-driven. If, on the other hand, you feel more at home in the left column with the classical verities, becoming event-driven may not be for you. You should seek your competitive advantage elsewhere.

Becoming Event-Driven:
The Ultimate IT Upgrade

Though most organizational change is presented in terms of shifts in human behavior, consultants have been discovering for years—as the former Coopers & Lybrand reengineering expert said in Chapter 1—that technology is responsible for 80 percent of successful, or unsuccessful, change. The company's human culture must change, too, of course, but if the tools aren't there, no amount of CEO oratory is going to accomplish the shift from old to new.

Information technology (IT) is today's prime driver of organizational change. Possessing and deploying superior information gives a company the kind of advantage the first riflemen had over archers at the Battle of Agincourt. But just as rifles, being new, inspired superstitious awe in medieval warriors (especially among archers), the novelty and power of today's information technology, though still in its clumsy infancy, sometimes dazzle its users into forgetting just why they're deploying information technology in the first place. Information technology is the key to competitive advantage *if it's the right technology for the job.*

Before you go shopping for IT solutions, forget about the machinery itself for a moment and consider the results you want to achieve. Only when you have goals and targets firmly in mind should you choose the technology to get you there. Making the change to event-driven should coincide exactly with your business strategy. You may want to get closer to your customers, or you may want to roll out an important new enterprise application and integrate it with all your other information sources.

Convene a small council of the best thinkers you can recruit from inside and outside the company, making sure to include the widest range of perspectives, from the chief information and financial officers to the chief of marketing communications to the wisest old and brashest new workers doing business on the customer interface. Don't be shy about inviting consultants to join the inner council: These are people with high-level, objective views of you and your competitors. Use their expertise. Opening the process could be your first step toward real change.

Using the company's vision as an unchanging guiding star, throw the floor wide open to suggestions for achieving that vision through change, reminding the group that there are no bad ideas. Part of the process is predictable: The world has been sufficiently oversold on the wonders of information technology that people who are not intimate with the actual workings of IT systems—the advertising and marketing folks, for example—will suggest miracles that are technically impossible to implement. The CIO will explain, quite rightly, that even the simplest systemic change is far more challenging and complex than it might at first seem. The consultants will propose solutions that will make the CFO blanch with sticker shock. Your job as leader is to remind the CFO that sticker shock is preferable to death by rust.

From this dialectic of thesis and antithesis will emerge a series of ultimate business goals that will define your need for upgraded information technology. Only then should you begin choosing the machinery to put those goals within your company's reach.

Your Dreams for Your Business

I hesitate to use the word "dreams" in a serious business book, but dreams, the waking kind, have become an important part of my professional life. People from outside the business world don't understand this, but you know it's true: If business leaders didn't have dreams (not plans, strategies, or goals) for their companies, they could never begin to put in the endless hours, leave families behind to travel the world, or lie awake nights searching for the one extra twist that elevates good to excellent. Money alone is not a sufficient motivator for that kind of behavior. The most satisfying part of my job is sitting with executives who harbor dreams for their companies, listening to their dreams, and then helping them come true through the inventive application of technology.

With that perspective in mind, allow me to discuss, briefly, some general attributes and attitudes of the event-driven company. See if they compare with the dreams you have for your company.

No More Islands of Information

The information technology upon which the event-driven company is based integrates into one shared system all the raw materials of knowledge residing in or circulating through the unconnected and previously uncommunicative mainframes, databases, client/server arrays, and applications in your organization. By converting information from the passive request/reply paradigm to proactive publish/subscribe, the event-driven company ubiquitously provides each employee with a comprehensive diet of real-time, constantly upgraded information custom-designed to center each worker's job around value creation. The event-driven infrastructure is designed to repeatedly call workers' attention to significant events until they are acted on, alerting people to deal with and exploit exceptional cases while leaving routine events to machines (thus, "management by exception"). There is no such thing in the event-driven company as "I'll sweep this one under the rug," or "Sorry, it fell through the cracks."

Getting Out in Front of the Data Glut

Contrary to the image one might conjure up of workers being constantly and automatically informed, the event-driven infrastructure does not assault workers with a torrent of crises to which they must counterreact defensively; rather, publish/subscribe enables innovative, creative responses to events as well as information-fueled invention that *anticipates* events. The event-driven system gathers real-time, tightly focused information from everywhere in the company's ecosphere, pumps it through numerous analytical applications, and delivers it to workers' desks as a multipurpose tool for the worker's use. In addition, through the use of a corporate portal, such a system can integrate this internal information with valuable external information—such as news and weather—that may effect a given project or decision.

All Open Systems, All the Time

While there is deceptive, lazy comfort in closed systems—"value chains," "supply chains," proprietary electronic data exchange systems, "*keiretsu*," and so on—there is far greater opportunity in open systems. The Internet is an open system. Today's business world is an open system. The event-driven technology infrastructure is based on opening closed and proprietary computer systems and applications and letting them talk, teach, and learn from one another. Though open systems offer little barrier-style protection from raging competitive storms, they level the playing field and make it accessible to all comers on a meritocratic basis.

As a cellular entity with the means to connect freely with any other entity in the global ecosphere, the event-driven company thrives on open systems. Its goal is to connect with as many top-tier entities as possible (as customers, suppliers, allies, or combinations of the three), develop long-term but open-ended value-creating relationships, and thereby embed its core competencies in other organizations that find the relationship increasingly valuable for both sides.

Agility, Flexibility, Longevity

Though the event-driven company has the technological flexibility and the hair-trigger willingness to switch allies and suppliers opportunistically, at a moment's notice, in the name of customer value, it prefers longevity in all its relationships. Longevity generates far more value than either impulsive novelty or rote loyalty. The event-driven company encourages and abets longevity by sharing its value-added, active information in what Don Peppers and Martha Rogers [25] call a "learning relationship" with all connected entities in the supply network, constantly upgrading the relationships' value in a continuous upgrade-loop process the Japanese call *keizan teian,* which yields ever-richer knowledge.

The End of Denial

A cynical friend recently suggested that instead of challenging themselves with self-improvement programs, people could more easily "solve" their problems simply by strengthening their denial. Denial is as powerfully destructive in business as in our personal and family lives, making it possible for people and institutions to deny obvious problems and avoid change until it's too late. The event-driven infrastructure dismantles denial, making it impossible to sweep anything under the rug and rendering unacceptable the statements "I don't want to hear about it," "I don't want to look," and "I must have missed that."

The event-driven company is based on truths plain as a face slap. It requires major cultural adjustments to immerse a company properly in such truths. Leaders are challenged to convince employees that hard truths are more valuable, over time, than soft prevarications. Leaders must demonstrate, for example, that trying something innovative and failing is superior to sticking with the mediocre status quo. Truth, event-driven style, means the end of company blamestorms. The question must never be "Whose fault is this?" but "How can we learn from this?" The real-time nature of event-driven feedback makes learning from failure not only swifter but less damaging: The company is aware of what's going wrong the moment it starts to go wrong, making immediate corrections for the customer while at the same time learning and disseminating a lesson to others inside the company.

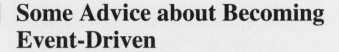

Some Advice about Becoming Event-Driven

I would have to spend weeks climbing around inside your company and listening to your dreams to offer accurate, specific advice on what to buy, whom to hire, what to change, what to lose, and what to keep as you become event-driven. No consultant should dare offer opinions without first knowing the client's business as well as the client. There are, however, certain issues and questions that occur in most conversions to event-driven, and on those issues I can offer advice.

What about ROI?

Let's say you decide your company should become event-driven. It will cost money, and, more wrenchingly, it will cost your organization the internal upheaval of accepting, adapting, and realigning to change. I'll go into the human element of becoming event-driven later, but for now let's talk about the easy cost: the money.

In deciding whether becoming event-driven is really "worth it," whether it delivers return on investment (ROI), there's the old argument to consider about the true impact on productivity of admittedly expensive IT investments. I believe debating productivity misses the main point. The real ROI advantage to becoming event-driven is *competitive*. On a primary level, solving your customers' problems in the emerging global and networked market requires real-time, integrated information. On a secondary level, if your competition is becoming event-driven and you're not, you're taking a big risk. In their book, *Enterprise One-to-One: Tools for Competing in the Interactive Age*, Peppers and Rogers [26] address a hypothetical CEO who's wondering whether the ROI for change is there:

Evaluate your investment based on the *strategic advantage* you can gain over your competitors, both current and future. Clearly, the more you invest in . . . knowledge-based systems the faster and more flexibly you'll operate your business. . . .

It is essential you do this before your competition does, because the advantage created may well be irreversible. If you are investing as much or more than your competitors, and provided you spend wisely, it is highly likely that your ROI will exceed 50 percent over just the first 18 months. If you invest much less than your competitors, then our suggestion is you should consider reducing your expenditures even further, because this might yield a higher return over the few years you can remain independent.

Becoming event-driven propels your company in the opposite direction from a strategy of cost cutting: I believe cutting costs as a strategy in itself is frequently ineffective. Companies that go out of business have no costs at all. There's also the ROI argument proffered by Santa Fe Institute economist Brian Arthur, who distinguishes between the "diminishing returns" of "resource-based bulk processing" and the world of "knowledge-based" "increasing returns." Arthur argues: "the ability to profit under increasing returns is only as good as the ability to see what is coming in the next cycle and to position oneself for it. . . . Success will strongly favor those who understand this new way of thinking" [27]. In my view, any company that becomes event-driven is positioned to enjoy "increasing returns," no matter its ostensible product.

And yet, having said all that, the dollar side of event-driven ROI remains an issue of importance to business leaders. On that subject, experience has confirmed the accuracy of the advice given by Peppers and Rogers [28]:

In analyzing your anticipated ROI, don't concentrate on next quarter's sales, or even the next year's. Instead, focus on the overall, long-term value of your customer base. If you have $100 million in annual profit and a reasonable amount of repurchase from your customers, for instance, then the actual value of your customer base (that is, the sum of all your customers' long-term value) might be several times this figure, perhaps . . . between $200 million and $1 billion. . . . If the [overall] value is, say, $400 million, then the question you want to consider is whether an investment in IT can grow the value of the customer base by, say, 5 percent, to $420 million. A $20 million increase in the value of your customer base will pay for a lot of microchips.

Best Practices of Consultants/Vendors

In 1985, on the eve of my first sale of an event-driven IT system, I noted four keys to success among information technology consultants who I felt were doing good work at that time. Interestingly, these characteristics, appropriately reshaped for today, now apply both to IT consultants who can help your company become event-driven and to event-driven companies themselves, in their relationships with *their* customers. I suggest you seek these four qualities in the consultants and vendors you bring aboard to help your company become event-driven:

1. Be a problem solver, not a technology vendor. Customers are frequently skeptical of new technology because of unpleasant past experiences. They have been sold solutions in a box and found they do not work as promised. To identify the customer's long-range strategic goals and day-to-day operational needs, put yourself in the customer's shoes and develop a deep understanding of the customer's business. Only then can technical solutions be proposed.

2. Recognize that the rate of migration toward a future ideal solution is limited by past decisions. Problems within a company can rarely be solved all at once, with all-new technology. There will usually be legacy systems that cannot be discarded. They must be integrated into any new solution. The best consultants solve problems working under constraints.

3. Understand that a true solution mixes the best, vendor-independent technologies. One cannot be both the customer's champion and the purveyor of just one company's wares, even one's own.

4. Practice sell-design-build. Consultant and customer create a true partnership when the customer displays commitment to a planned solution by providing early funding and other development support. Building solutions to meet specific customer problems, as opposed to building solutions and then looking for problems to solve with them, avoids waste of time and money.

There's one more crucial ingredient that has been paramount in my experience from the very beginning: Complex technological change can rarely succeed unless there are strategically placed, battle-ready champions for change *inside* the customer's company.

No matter how enthusiastically a company embraces the concept of change in the beginning, the inevitable wear and tear of routine disruption, cultural uncertainties, fearful resistance to the new, the sudden appearance of steep learning curves, and, in some cases, mounting expenses will eventually bring the project to a point where internal approval must be won all over again. The best salesmanship and the most collegial consulting relationship will mean little at this moment. The crucial battle will be fought within the company, behind closed doors. Unless there are committed evangelists for change in the board room, in the executive suite, and on the company's customer interface, this new, go-ahead-and-finish-the-job approval may be hard to win.

If you are a manager planning to become event-driven, it's imperative that you recruit and empower champions of change at every significant pressure point in your company. Share your plans with these champions, honor their views, put the latest information in their hands to use as weapons against the forces of stasis. Be inspired by the thought that once your company has successfully become event-driven, every worker will receive the same special treatment. Each will know the company's plans in depth. Each will have his or her views honored. Each will have the latest information to use as weapons against the forces of rust.

Throughout this chapter, primarily as a rhetorical device, I've presented the "option" of achieving competitive advantage by becoming event-driven. In point of fact, as Peppers and Rogers [29] point out at the end of their book:

> . . . this kind of change is not optional. It [is] inevitable. When the dust settles, the odds are that the winner won't be you but some totally new enterprise—one with no stake at all in the current system.
>
> If you want to beat the odds, if you want your company to prosper in the Interactive Age, then . . . embrace the capabilities that technology now makes possible. . . . It's a lengthy, difficult process, a long voyage far from shore. . . . *Make* it happen. Don't wait for it to happen to you. And good luck on the voyage.

CHAPTER **3**

FROM THE TRADING FLOOR TO THE EVENT-DRIVEN ENTERPRISE

The Event-Driven Warrior

Becoming event-driven unifies a company's collective aware-ness so that the whole organization, no matter how global or distributed, reacts as an individual organism that adapts to changes in the environment in line with a shared and unified vi-sion. The original event-driven organism was one individual: the smartest, strongest hunter who saw prey first and was the fastest in the group to pounce on and devour it.

Of all business professionals, the financial trader is the clos-est to being purely event-driven. The trading floor is one of the most information-intensive environments in the world, and it was for the trader that we first developed real-time infrastruc-ture software. The complex, integrated, value-added market in-formation dancing across the video screen of the trader your broker looks to for instant order execution arrives at the trader's station via publish/subscribe technology. Your trader learns about every flicker in stock and bond prices as they're happen-ing, *and* what those flickers mean. His or her lightning-quick *event-driven reaction* to change is an excellent example of how instant information drives instant innovation.

In fact, if the event-driven infrastructure can be said to have a single transformational goal for your company, it is to give ev-ery single employee the tools to become more trader-like—hyper-aware, entrepreneurial, fully informed about every shift and trend in the competitive environment.

Several times I've mentioned "value-added information." In the event-driven infrastructure's earlier days, in the 1980s, we sought to create extra customer value by augmenting the simple reporting of fluctuations in stock prices by feeding those price-change reports into application programs that used them to cre-ate wide-ranging analyses or automated trading decisions. These higher functions in turn created new data, which we in-stantaneously fed back into the network for other traders to use. The result was an upward-spiraling, endless-feedback loop of constantly, incrementally enriched, refined, and integrated in-formation, a variant of the *keizan teian* never-ending upgrade process. The strategic application of this loop in executing and improving any number of business processes is a prime competitive advantage of the event-driven company. That advantage will grow as the world becomes universally networked and more and more processes—in and out of the financial sector—become completely automated. The richer, faster, and more on point the information driving these automated functions, the more value companies will derive.

When I witnessed how the *keizan teian* feedback loop and other event-driven capabilities drove successes on the financial trading floor, I realized that integrated, real-time information would create ever-richer customer value in all businesses, not just the financial markets. After all, the world we all work in is becoming as wired for communications and as speed obsessed as a stock exchange. Thanks to the growth of the Internet and of corporate networks—the infrastructure that undergirds the event-driven infrastructure—many businesses in fields other than finance have become event-driven and are now creating superior customer value in spheres as diverse as manufacturing, construction, consumer electronics, petrochemicals, high technology, and the Internet itself.

Different industries use the event-driven architecture to realize different benefits. Construction giant Bechtel, as we've seen, uses a global event-driven infrastructure to reduce costly delays that previously allowed competitors to underbid jobs. The majority of the world's largest microchip manufacturers use event-driven technology to monitor and manage their complex chip fabrication processes. Database companies such as Oracle, Sybase, and Informix have added event-driven features to their databases to create active catalogs whose information can be combined with other data, analyzed, and pushed to the workers who need it. Networking leaders Cisco and 3Com are using the event-driven infrastructure to provide more reliable, cost-effective, and bandwidth-friendly data through private networks and the public Internet. Motorola's pager division delivers customized pagers, which can be shipped from around the globe in record time. Oil and energy companies utilize publish/subscribe to track the buying, selling, and transport of raw materials on a global scale. I'm sure you can imagine many ways your company could apply the benefits of becoming event-driven.

And it all began on the trading floor . . .

Trading: The Oldest Human Profession

Despite the old adage, *trading* may, in fact, be the oldest human profession. People have been trading for thousands of years, and it is deeply ingrained in our species' awareness. In more modern terms, trading is one of the purest value-creating, rust-resistant industries. Although the clerical act of buying and selling securities is a commodity, trading at the highest level is 100 percent knowledge-based and cannot, at least for the moment, be commoditized. Automation has yet to surpass, much less equal, the trading skills of an intelligent human armed with the right information. In addition to skill, of course, the successful trader relies on speed to capture his or her prey. This requisite mixture of complex thinking and speedy execution made it clear to me from the very beginning that in trading, as practiced in the world's financial markets, I would find fertile and receptive ground for developing and creating the event-driven company.

"Complexity and speed do not mix," argues Christopher Meyer [30] in *Fast Cycle Time: How to Align Purpose, Strategy, and Structure for Speed*, but I disagreed—as I also disagree, incidentally, with the start/stop concept of cycles themselves; we're all doing business on one endless cycle now—and was convinced that the right mixture of complexity and speed would be the main ingredient of success on a trading floor.

Experience over the past 15 years has confirmed my early theoretical belief that finance—because of its reliance on information, information systems, the logic of information flow, and split-second execution—is an excellent predictive microcosm of economic trends that flower five or ten years later in the general economy. Before the words "Internet," "intranet," or "client/server" entered much of the world's awareness, stock exchanges and brokerages were heavily wired with information technology networks *and* the problems inherent in such passive, request/reply systems.

The Tower of Information Babel (or more appropriately Babble) I encountered on the investment bank trading floor precisely predicted one of the greatest problems now afflicting the Internet: multiple content sources combining with many content consumers to create overwhelming confusion, a situation that cries out for a fast, high-efficiency system to manage the content pouring in from all those sources to all those users. I'm not exaggerating when I say that some traders in the mid-1980s and for years afterward were forced to ply their trade from 25 different, technologically incompatible sources of news and analysis delivered to as many as 18 separate monitors (with three or more keyboards) stacked on and around their desks.

Just as finance itself is predictive on the macro level, on an individual level the financial trader is also a bellwether. By nature the market trader should be event-driven to the bone: hungry, cunning, intelligent, strong, and quick enough to pounce on prey before his or her fellows. Yet, when I first encountered the financial trader of the middle 1980s at the world's leading investment banks (IBs), it was hard to find that sleek, speedy, competitive warrior beneath layers of complacency from 40 years of uninterrupted prosperity, national insularity, and protective government regulation. Alarmingly for the investment bankers, all the rules of the game were changing at once at the time we met. Reassuringly, when I met Goldman Sachs they were wise enough to realize they needed to change to capitalize on the new, emerging financial services industry.

Until the early 1980s, the trading departments of IBs realized most of their profits by charging investors commissions for finding matches, or "crosses," between those who wanted to sell investment instruments and those who wanted to buy. The padded commissions were set by federal regulation at astronomical levels, as much as 75 cents per share. The American investing community represented a small, placid slice of the population— large institutions and affluent individuals—who put their money into American stocks and tended to keep them there. Market automation was stuck at the 20-year-old, five-million-share-a-day levels, making the mere execution of the simplest transactions slow and expensively labor-intensive.

Then, suddenly, everything was different. Commission-protecting government regulations ended. Discount brokers appeared. Profitable opportunities beckoned to investors from overseas. Investors, for their part, started demanding higher-value, custom-tailored products, such as options.

As corporate pension systems disappeared in the reengineering of the period and the public lost faith in the ability of Social Security to cushion retirement, popular mutual funds arose that drew the average person into the markets, a trend that has yet to peak. Americans have a greater share of their money in the stock market now than at any time in the past 50 years, according to a February 1998 *New York Times* [31] analysis of Federal Reserve statistics. For the first time ever, the *Times* reported, Americans have more money invested in stocks than in their homes.

Though infrastructured for 1960s-era, five-million-share days, the New York Stock Exchange by the mid-1980s was routinely experiencing 100-million-share days. The old administration and reporting machinery was groaning under the load. (On October 28, 1997, 1.2 *billion* shares of stock changed hands on the NYSE without melting down the financial system.) The leisurely days were gone forever. Speed was now king and killer.

Here was a textbook case of instant commoditization. The IBs' trading margins didn't so much shrink as evaporate. Finding "crosses" was no longer enough, and Robert Rubin knew it. In 1985, Rubin, later to become secretary of the treasury, headed Goldman Sachs's equities trading department. Anticipating the future before his competitors, Rubin realized that the financial services ecosystem in general and Goldman Sachs in particular were obliged to reinvent themselves or perish in a ruststorm of commoditization. He knew it was time to reawaken the warrior in his traders.

85 Broad Street

The Goldman Sachs Warrior of today, Currency Trader model, rises before dawn: 5:14 A.M., to be exact, awakened by the twin murmurs of all-news radio WINS and CNBC-TV. The business news is all Asia. The *Financial Times* says today will be about numbers: payroll, unemployment, GDP. *And* it's triple-witching day. The Warrior checks his pager, grins to see that overnight currency rates have moved in his favor. He senses profit. Subway to 85 Broad Street in the neighborhood known as Wall Street, elevator to 26, Goldman's New York trading floor, mutual battleground for 450 fellow members of the tribe. At 6:45 A.M. the elevator delivers the Warrior into a large, airy room with a suspended, golden-wood ceiling, and thick, men's club navy–carpet underfoot. Many of the Warriors who work in this room earn in the seven figures, yet their desks are cramped closer together than secretaries' desks in an old-fashioned typing pool. There's a low hum of controlled but excited voices in the room, and the recording-studio aroma of solid-state electronics.

On each desk sit two 25-inch computer monitors, powered by a Sun SPARC workstation. One of the monitors, displaying a complex data reporting and analysis package called Market-Sheet, is a tightly packed, constantly changing grid of various colored charts, graphs, lists, and moving "crawls" of breaking news (Figure 3.1). The effect suggests a British railroad timetable redesigned by an MTV producer with a Ph.D. in quantum physics: every piece of text and illustration in constant blinking, undulating motion. Various sections of the screen blip different colors every few seconds as they shape-shift to reflect real-time updates. The Warrior's second desktop monitor displays internal Goldman Sachs applications, trading analyses, e-mail, and an Internet browser. There's a digital turret phone with 100 lines on every desk, lights flashing constantly as other traders and customers seek to reach the Warrior. His biggest decision at any given moment is which line to answer. Which line promises to deliver the most profit?

■ ■ ■ ■

Figure 3.1

Marketsheet
for Windows
screen shot.

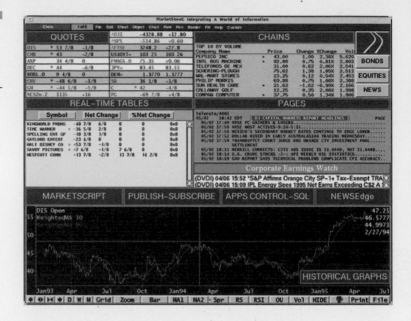

It's 6:47 A.M. Goldman's London traders have handed off to
New York. Later, New York will hand off to Tokyo. Trading
continues worldwide, 24 hours per day. The Warrior's Market-
Sheet displays news summaries—Asia on the left, Europe on
the right, United States across the bottom. The analyst who spe-
cializes in British pounds sterling, the Warrior's specialty, an-
nounces predictions for the day: "50/60 should be the high."

"50" refers to the buy and "60" to the sell quotes for the British pound sterling against the dollar. The number is short for
"$1.6350 buy, $1.6360 sell." The traders don't even mention the
$1.63 part of the rate. Millions in profit or loss reside in the
mills: the amounts worth less than one cent.

The Warrior, a phone at each ear, hears a subtle alarm ring
from the MarketSheet, calling attention to the news viewer window on the screen. It's been programmed to beep when any
news concerning British pounds sterling crosses the wires.
Reuters reports the Bank of England is buying sterling. Knight-
Ridder, a competing news provider, reports the German and
Financial Times exchange rates moving in response to the Bank

of England intervention. Reuters again: "BofE denies today's actions are the results of inflation concerns."

Before plunging into the action, the Warrior takes a moment to execute a routine task and clicks on a button marked "Reports." Automatically, MarketSheet assembles charts, analyses, and commentary from Goldman Sachs's European affiliates into a two-page newsletter and faxes copies to all clients. This daily bit of marketing used to take the Warrior an hour each morning.

7:26 A.M.: A client, a giant oil multinational, orders $100 million in pounds sterling to meet payroll in the United Kingdom. If the Warrior can buy the sterling low and sell it to the client at a price that's just a bit higher but still fair, there's profit in it. A few desks down, another trader in the sterling department yells out, "I have a seller! Anybody take a hundred?" by which he means $100 million in British currency. His eyes darting between two segments of the MarketSheet screen—one showing who's buying sterling around the world and who's selling, the other flashing continuously as real-time price updates arrive—the Warrior starts buying: "I'll take 40 (million) at 50 ($1.6350 per £1)." The price stays the same on the screen. "I'll take 20 at 50." The price stays the same. "I'll take 40 at 50." He's now bought $100 million worth of currency in five seconds.

In a side office off the trading floor, a beeping alert—an example of the event-driven infrastructure's "management by exception"—draws the attention of Goldman Sachs's currency risk manager. A risk-analysis report window is blinking on his MarketSheet monitor. The Warrior, he sees, has bought $100 million of sterling before 8:00 A.M. What if the price of sterling drops lower? Goldman won't be able to sell the currency to its oil company client for an acceptable margin. The risk manager types out a warning that pops up on all sterling traders' screens: Watch your exposure folks. It's still early in the move. Following a prompt from MarketSheet, the risk manager drags and drops the Warrior and his sterling position into his "watch" list, where it joins other "watch" situations unfolding around the room, their displays prioritized for the risk manager in a preprogrammed hierarchy, similar to planes awaiting their turns to land. If the price of sterling goes below 50 or the Warrior buys more, an alarm will sound and the risk manager will intervene.

8:01 A.M.: The Warrior, in a few-second lull between trades, clicks on "P&L" to check his personal performance, tied directly into his bonus. Looking good so far.

9:30 A.M.: Across the room, pandemonium breaks out at the equities desks as takeover rumors send the arbitrage guys into a frenzy. The Warrior is old enough to remember back a few years, when the arbitrageurs stood in front of stacks of unconnected data screens, calculating wildly by the seats of their pants—overbought, oversold, volatilities, recommendations. Now MarketSheet runs the models and analyses for them, automatically pointing out arbitrage opportunities.

10 A.M.: A green flash of light from the screen. The Warrior's little joke: He's set his news filter to flash green whenever the news crawl contains the words "Alan Greenspan." Now the Fed chairman's comments scroll across the MarketSheet news window, followed moments later by scurrying analyst opinion and trade recommendations.

10:01 A.M.: Greenspan has spoken. Market turbulence ensues. Now the Warrior surfs market volatility. MarketSheet flashes a sterling quote—buying at 55. He sells some that he bought at 50, watching his P&L score on the monitor go up instantly.

4:00 P.M.: Time to "pass the book" to the Tokyo office. Later, Tokyo will pass it to London, then back to 85 Broad Street again. The sun never sets on the Goldman Sachs trading empire. Drained but sated, the Warrior sets MarketSheet to page him automatically on the cell if sterling breaks 60. Then he puts down his weapons for the day.

The Way It Was

"I'm not going to talk to you about technology," I promised Robert Rubin when I first met him through a business connection in late 1985. "I'd simply like to understand your business."

A few days later, I took the elevator at 85 Broad Street to 27 (one floor above today's trading area) and was astonished by the scene I encountered. In a room where information and speed could make or lose hundreds of millions of dollars, the traders' systems seem to have been designed for a more sedate pace of business.

I've mentioned that the traders drew their information from as many as 25 competing information sources (Dow-Jones, Reuters, etc.), most of which were delivered in proprietary, technically incompatible formats. Moreover, highly paid traders were forced to act as clerks: It took over 20 separate keyboard entries to record the specific details of one customer buying a security.

The room looked like a computer store's disarrayed warehouse. Monitors were piled everywhere. Thick braids of cable wound under desks and across the carpet. I learned later that if one cable were accidentally unplugged—not uncommon in that jumble—several neighboring screens went dead, too, in the midst of trading frenzy. Electric fans whirred on each desk to keep the machines cool. The traders had to weight their flapping papers to avoid having them blown away. Each trader had his or her own personalized array of computers, screens, and keyboards (the traders gamely tried to organize their information flow themselves), so when a trader moved desks, the IT staff had to unplug the entire construction and reassemble it across the room. This custodial task was one of the few that actually brought Goldman Sachs's information technology experts to the floor. As Rubin later told me, the trading systems had been designed with a mainframe mentality by people who had never spent time on the trading floor.

There was an enormous disconnect in that room between the kind of information traders needed and the way it was provided to them. Traders specializing in technical stocks, for example, were interested only in news about IBM, Apple, Digital Equipment, Intel, Oracle, and so on. But the sources sending data to the traders' screens didn't organize news that way. Each content provider just threw everything into its "feed" and left it to the traders to filter what they needed from the rush of unorganized statistics on their massed monitors, and then turn that clumsily gathered information into useful knowledge. Perversely, this awful system got worse at precisely the moment traders needed it most: During moments of greatest market volatility, when danger and opportunity presented themselves in dancing, evanescent micromoments, the reporting system would collapse under the weight of its own inefficiency.

Watching the traders wrestle their tools to do their jobs, I realized how much more they could accomplish if all these disconnected, incommunicado islands of data could be connected to one another and the resulting data mass shaped to deliver exactly the information each trader needed in the form that would provide the greatest value. It would amplify value even more if traders could feed their customized information through analytical, decision-support applications that adjusted relationally in real time, offering sets of appropriate actions and reactions and projected "what-if" scenarios, and then reported on the system-wide impact of the actions traders took. Though the phrase had not yet been born, what Goldman Sachs's trading floor badly needed to gain an advantage over its competitors was to become event-driven.

The anarchy raging on Goldman Sachs's trading floor presented a textbook problem for a distributed-computing solution I'd been mulling and developing for some time. To make the trading floor event-driven, market data from the competing, incompatible news services had to be made available in a common format or language. Then, the data had to be driven through other applications to create analytical results. All participants in the system should be equipped to recirculate to all other participants both the upgraded information they had received and processed and reports of any actions they had taken that would affect the information. Information would pass through one generation of refinement and usefulness after another.

I was convinced we could reduce the jumble of monitors to a single screen if we designed the display carefully and allowed traders to customize their own view of the data individually.

How the Trading Floor Eventually Became Event-Driven

I'd like to be able report that Goldman Sachs leaped immediately aboard my vision and the result was today's event-driven trading floor, as represented by the Warrior and his Market-Sheet. It happened eventually, but there were a number of detours and false starts along the way. Among them was some politics and resistance to the changes wrought by the event-driven infrastructure.

What we proposed for Goldman Sachs was a distributed system in which, rather than dumb terminals connected to the mainframe, each trader would have his or her own networked personal workstation manufactured by a new company called Sun Microsystems. Goldman worried, however, that Sun wouldn't have market staying power and was hesitant to invest in a solution reliant on potentially transient technology. In addition, their mainframe mentality argued that workstations would never equal the processing power of the mainframe. Our differing visions resulted in a several-year lapse between when we first proposed the event-driven digital trading floor to Goldman and when Goldman Sachs did become event-driven, and the Warrior on the 26th floor got his MarketSheet. The pioneering event-driven breakthrough actually came elsewhere despite Goldman's contribution to discovering the solution.

Our Break at Fidelity

After our disappointment at Goldman Sachs, good fortune gave us a chance to present the event-driven concept to Fidelity Investments in 1987, when the venerable firm was designing a new fixed-income trading floor. Our unproven little group was given a last-minute, uphill opportunity to change the firm's positive mindset about Reuters, the established market leader in trading-floor data delivery, with whom Fidelity was about to sign a contract.

Having failed to convince Goldman Sachs with *theoretical* arguments in 1985, I'd spent much of the intervening two years developing what I hoped were dramatic *demonstrations* of the event-driven structure's potential. Would they be dramatic enough to divert Fidelity from signing with Reuters? Allow me to give you some important background on the technology we were about to present.

Two central features of the event-driven architecture that we had been perfecting in the years between the failure at Goldman Sachs and the Fidelity opportunity are The Information Bus (TIB) and publish/subscribe information delivery via subject-based addressing (both components of our current real-time infrastructure strategy for both the enterprise and the Internet). Briefly stated, TIB is to software what the familiar "bus" is to hardware—a central, universal conduit into which components and applications can be plugged so that, regardless of their language or technology, they will communicate and interoperate. By translating into TIBspeak all 25 incompatible market-data sources that flowed onto the trading floor, we were able to mix and match the specific data each trader needed; let the data act upon one another; and then present the dynamic, *keizan teian* results on a single monitor screen. But how did we know exactly what the traders needed to know, and, having figured that out, how could we deliver it?

The answer is publish/subscribe via subject-based addressing, in which an electronic message is addressed by its *content* rather than its *recipient* and then delivered (published) to any computer whose operator has "subscribed" to the information (Figure 3.2). Instead of an e-mail addressed to "joe@great-co.com" and destined for Joe alone, a subject-addressed publish/subscribe message is "addressed" to a subject and goes to everyone in an organization who has subscribed to that subject. A message about the real-time price of IBM stock, for example, is addressed "equities.ibm.nyse," and everyone who has expressed an interest in the price of IBM stock, by subscribing, gets the message instantly.

We built demos that would demonstrate these technologies in a captivating fashion. One demo was a mock business plan for a hypothetical multinational corporation. The other was a "living

Figure 3.2
Market data
distribution
system.

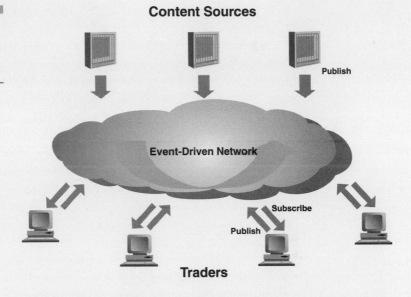

index card"—crude forerunner of the MarketSheet—designed to give an equities trader everything he or she needed and wanted to know about one security, in this case IBM.

The business plan demo consisted of a word processing program displaying the business plan itself, a spreadsheet outlining projected P&L, a database with mocked-up figures from the company's imagined operations, and a graphics program presenting illustrative charts and graphs. We identified a single variable: the cost of labor in each of the various countries where the company planned to do business. Then we tagged the information with the subject "labor.rate" and had each of the applications "subscribe" to the message "labor.rate."

As we moved from country to country and reported each nation's wage structure over a mocked-up data-delivery service, application programs received the data contained in "labor.rate" and changed their reports relationally in real time. Before our potential customers' eyes, the word processing program changed the business plan's paragraphs quoting the labor rates and projecting profit margins that depended on the prevailing cost of labor. The spreadsheet changed P&L projections in real time as wages changed at borders. The database reacted to a shift in wages with instant shifts in affected categories. And the charts and graphs reconfigured themselves to reflect the new projections.

Then we unveiled the "living index card." Here was our chance to use our information technology to integrate and present information the way traders needed to have it, correct the reigning disconnect between information requirements and information delivery techniques, and thus revolutionize the trading floor. No longer would traders twist themselves like human pretzels simply to glean the market data and analysis needed to do their jobs. We were determined to place the requirements of people above the dictates of machines.

We researched every conceivable subsequent action and reaction that would be triggered by changes in the price of a stock. Then, blending and collating live (not mocked-up) data streaming in from 25 incompatible news-reporting sources, we presented coherent, real-time reports on the stock's price alongside simultaneous real-time reports, in text and charts, tracking the outward-rippling impact of each potential trading action. For the first time anywhere, a trader (albeit a hypothetical one) had all the information he or she needed to create maximum value, delivered instantaneously to a single monitor.

The effect on the Fidelity executives was galvanizing. The Fidelity people were "blown away" by the demos. The executives had been skeptical of our promises, but here was proof. Though one top manager had warned us the firm would never order technology that was not already installed and working elsewhere, we received on the spot an order that led to a 60-position installation for Fidelity's fixed-income trading floor.

This installation was the first to bypass the mainframe and use the Sun desktop workstations that Goldman Sachs had been so concerned about. Fidelity immediately decided to put the Reuters contract on hold while we installed a pilot project.

Beyond the Trading Floor

In the beginning, it was a struggle to convince the world's most aggressive financial trading companies that they could acquire a competitive advantage by successfully blending speed with an entirely new form of self-refining knowledge integrated from diverse, previously incompatible information sources. Since those early days, the event-driven architecture has become predominant in the world's financial markets and is fast becoming so in the enterprise and on the Internet as well.

As I said earlier, what happens in financial trading surfaces years later in other industries, and that is precisely the case right now. Where once only financial players lived or died on their ability to blend complexity with speed, now all companies are called upon to do precisely that to simply hold commoditization at bay. Where once only financial traders were sufficiently wired to become event-driven, today most companies are strengthening their networks and Internet strategies as they prepare to do battle in the global networked economy.

The victors, I believe, will be those companies that adopt the event-driven infrastructure and arm each employee with what it takes to become a trader/warrior, using integrated, value-added information to extend his or her perceptions and knowledge to the borders of what can be known about the business environment. Equipping employees with event-driven information constantly reminds all your people that the profit and loss of the company rests in their hands, and every moment is a distinct opportunity either seized for the benefit of the home team or lost to the competition.

Now it's time to peek under the hood of the event-driven infrastructure.

CHAPTER 4

THE EVENT-DRIVEN IT ARCHITECTURE

From the Trading Floor to the Enterprise to the Internet

On February 10, 1998, Cisco Systems, Inc., and TIBCO announced Pragmatic General Multicast (PGM), a new networking protocol for reliably transmitting information to many locations on a network simultaneously. (TIBCO worked with Cisco in the development of this protocol.) That's a pretty dry description, but the impact of multicasting on corporate networks and the Internet will be anything but dry.

The top-line immediate benefit of multicasting is that by reshaping the flow of information it will increase the capacity of existing network bandwidth–on intranets and the Internet–by a factor of at least 10. Moreover, the extra reliability of PGM will, for the first time, open the Internet to universally trustworthy e-commerce.

Customers were using the Internet to buy products and trade on a retail level long before PGM, but institutions predicated on numerical exactitude–investment banks and other global enterprises–preferred not to use the Internet because of its technical unreliability. PGM solves the reliability problem.

PGM's introduction to the Internet will complete the successful evolution of the event-driven infrastructure from the trading floor to the enterprise to the Internet. The event-driven paradigm, developed nearly 15 years ago as a narrowly vertical solution in a uniquely information-intensive environment, now has the potential to change the direction of the World Wide Web as the world itself becomes an information-intensive environment. Having earned the endorsement of such market drivers as Cisco and Sun, multicasting promises to convert the Internet itself into an event-driven environment.

"The Internet needs multicasting. You need multicasting. This is the year you might finally get it," wrote Jesse Berst [32], editorial director of the Ziff-Davis Network, in his online column of February 9, 1998, hailing the introduction of PGM. "Multicasting sends a single data stream, which is then forwarded to everyone who wants it. Unicasting—the method used today on the Internet—sends a separate data stream to each person. If 1 million people want a big, fat multimedia file, that file will be sent 1 million times. Now do you see why the Internet is clogged? *We can never throw enough bandwidth at congestion problems to solve them.*" (italics added)

That message has not penetrated all quarters. A few days later, on February 12, the *San Francisco Chronicle* [33] reported that Internet service providers (ISPs) would soon raise access fees due to multiplying demand for user bandwidth. The *Chronicle* quoted John Sidgmore, chief operating officer of World-Com, one of the largest Internet "backbone" operators: "In three years we're planning on having a network that's 1,000 times bigger than our current network. If you're not scared by this, you don't understand the situation."

Sidgmore's comment scared me, but not for the reason he intended. By building a 1,000 times larger network without upgrading his view of how information should flow over that network, Sidgmore is *paving a cowpath*, one of the worst mistakes a technology leader can make. "Paving a cowpath" is a figure of speech employed by reengineering authority Michael Hammer.

By "paving cowpaths," Hammer refers to the reflex habit of early American road builders, who poured molten macadam on existing cowpaths rather than exploit the capabilities of new technology to imagine fresh ways to get people where they wanted to go. Building an Internet backbone 1,000 times bigger than what we have now without thinking about new ways to use existing bandwidth is a perfect example of paving a cowpath (about ten feet deep in macadam!) and, as Hammer might argue, embedding outdated processes in silicon and software. The Internet as it exists today could immediately accommodate at least ten times more traffic by switching from unicasting to multicasting. With Internet usage in the United States alone doubling every 100 days, we will certainly need more bandwidth. But it is foolish to build bigger backbones without also exploiting the bandwidth-saving capabilities of multicasting.

Sidgmore's plan to build networks 1,000 times larger than what we have today rather than heeding Jesse Berst's admonition—"We can never throw enough bandwidth at congestion problems to solve them"—graphically illustrates the largest challenge to leadership in converting any company from contemporary to event-driven: abandoning the comfortable, familiar paved cowpaths and, as Hammer suggests, "starting fresh." This was true for the trading floor, where the event-driven solution encountered resistance from the defenders of mainframe-based batch analysis. It is true in enterprises outside the financial ecosystem, where the ingrained acceptance of the client/server paradigm is slowing the conversion of passive, isolated information into active, integrated, event-driven information.

The Internet, happily, may be a different story, for several reasons. No one "owns" the Internet, which makes it closer to a complex/chaotic data democracy—relatively free of cowpaths to pave—in which better ideas are more quickly accepted. The Internet community prides itself on embracing speed, which also lubricates the progress of innovation. Finally, the Internet's major commercial players have been receptive to our years of evangelizing the benefits of multicasting. I'm optimistic that the Internet's conversion to event-driven multicasting will be swift and smooth.

Because it promises to change the nature and vastly expand the leisure-time and commercial capabilities of the world's largest public network, the Internet, the publish/subscribe technology known as multicasting may become the most widely known element of the event-driven architecture. It is, however, only one element of many. As with all the other elements, multicasting delivers a major strategic benefit through the application of nuts-and-bolts, sweat-and-guts information technology. It is my aim in this chapter to describe in detail the nuts and bolts of each element of the event-driven architecture and explain each part's contribution to the overall goal of the event-driven organization: to deliver to every member of the organization the active, integrated information he or she must have to create maximum value for customers, the company and its allies, and the worker.

That's the goal. The basic *value* of the event-driven company is to change the very nature of information from passive cargo that arrives, when queried, via paved cowpath, to an active enzyme that circulates throughout an ecosphere in which all points are instantly accessible from all other points.

▇▇ ▇▇ Information Is Knowledge Is Power

The more one understands the technology of computerized information-flow systems, the more daunting seem the challenges of delivering active information where and when it is needed and circulating active information through a universally accessible ecosphere. Such achievements require extensive cross-integration of complex processes, widely disparate machines, and a bewildering profusion of application programs that, in the non-event-driven world, simply cannot communicate. It is the event-driven architecture's job to enable full-multiplex communication among these incompatible elements.

While writing this chapter, I met with the CIO of a major computer manufacturer to plan how it could use event-driven technology to speed up its order management process. It's business process included a concept called "available to promise." When a customer says, "Great. This package of solutions solves my problem. I want this," The company tells the customer when to expect delivery. It sounds simple, but there are so many steps between "I want it," and "Sure: It'll be there March 29," that it originally took weeks to fix "available to promise" dates. The company worked hard to squeeze out as much delay as possible and eventually reduced the lag between order and "available to promise" to a matter of hours. But this heroic advance was not enough to satisfy its customers, especially since such competitors as Dell were also shrinking their order processing cycle with an eye toward reducing it to zero.

People who order PCs are accustomed to doing business on the Internet. They want to order now and get their "available to promise" date in real time, while they wait. With PCs themselves having become undifferentiated commodities, PC customers will give their business to the company that can serve them in real time.

To deliver "available to promise" in real time, a manufacturer needs event-driven technology to communicate with its multiple suppliers instantly and reorganize the various processes that lie between order and "available to promise" from sequential to simultaneous. Compounding the technical challenge, customers insist that the company's real-time "available to promise" systems be running and reliable 24 hours a day, seven days a week.

Elements of a real-time "available to promise" infrastructure deliver the following:

- Real-time reports of sales and production data pushed as they are generated to those who need them (i.e., salespeople, operations staff, and business managers).

- Real-time "data marts" that contain up-to-the-moment content on the business and its performance. Anyone who has tried to implement non-real-time data mart or data warehousing knows that the mart or warehouse is good for historical analysis only, because its snapshot of the business is always out of date. A real-time data mart provides a cross-section of the business in the current moment.

- Increased value from packaged applications (such as those from SAP), because the information they manage is now more accessible and the applications themselves are easier to connect to other related applications.

The goal in integrating manufacturing processes is to cross-link every process, application, data source, and subcell within the organization so each can communicate, "teach," and "learn" from one another in real time and give the customer "available to promise" instantly. Though no single piece of information in the system is particularly exciting—"The customer has poor credit. Request a 50 percent advance deposit," "The factory will receive disk drives in three days," "Make sure ten extra workers are added to the morning crew next Thursday," "The cargo ship from Taiwan will not arrive in time. Have the needed parts shipped by air," "The price of DRAM memory has just dropped. We can offer a 10 percent discount"—in the aggregate this information, properly activated, becomes a potential competitive advantage for manufacturing and other companies.

In today's business environment, active information is the basic ingredient of value creation. In his influential book, *Intellectual Capital: The New Wealth of Organizations*, Thomas A. Stewart [34] notes that information used to support the "real" business; but now it *is* the real business. What was once true only for such "pure knowledge" industries as financial trading is now true for all companies that hope to survive and prosper in the age of instant commoditization. If you are not in the knowledge business today, you will not be in business tomorrow. "In the new economic era," writes Stewart, "wealth is the product of knowledge. Knowledge and information—not just scientific knowledge, but news, advice, entertainment, communication, service—have become the economy's most important products. Knowledge is what we buy and sell."

Stewart advises business leaders to "focus on the flow of information, not the flow of materials." From my earliest days studying electrical engineering at MIT and business administration at Harvard, I knew that changing the existing logic and methods of information flow, as Stewart suggests, would trigger a revolution. In practical terms, this meant creating an architecture that activates information—regardless of where it resides on a network, in what language it's written, on what platform it runs—adds intelligence to it, and brings it to life so that it ripples throughout the company's value ecosystem and returns, enriched, as knowledge that seeks out those who need it. This information architecture lies at the heart of the event-driven company. And at the heart of that architecture lies the publish/subscribe model for information exchange.

The Publish/Subscribe Paradigm

The vast majority of business information systems, whether on corporate networks or the Internet, work on the "request/reply," or "pull" model. Anyone seeking information must find out where the information is stored and then request it in just the right manner to trigger a reply. Each request for information is queued and then individually fulfilled by the provider (a Web page or an enterprise application). Once the seeker finds the network location of what he or she needs, learns how to phrase the request properly to trigger a reply, and waits his or her turn in the queue, there's still no guarantee that the information delivered will be fresh or usefully refined. Witness the flotsam served up by Internet search engines.

Futility and frustration are not the only by-products of request/reply. Networks become clogged because many individuals are simultaneously "polling" databases or Web sites as they root around for information they hope is there somewhere. Even when information's location is known, if 5,000 people request the data, these data must repeat themselves 5,000 times in reply. Imagine the melt-down effect of everyone in your town telephoning the recorded time announcement at the same moment.

Realizing the limitations of pure request/reply but not understanding how radically the paradigm needed to be changed, some developers in the late 1990s introduced "automated pull," or "automated polling," and inaccurately called it "push" computing. The media accepted the false "push" label. This was a short-lived and, in the long term, counter-productive marketing "triumph." As confirmed by a February 16, 1998, *New York Times* [35] article headlined "Push, the Hot Technology of '97, Gets a Cold Shoulder in '98," consumers soon felt burned by the promises fake push, quite predictably, failed to keep.

Fake push "channels," for example, behaved less like pinpoint data-delivery systems and more like out-of-control search engines, routinely filling customers' hard drives with garbage. Ziff-Davis's Jesse Berst [36] describes the result: "Imagine if the paperboy dumped 200 magazines onto your front porch every single morning."

Using automated polling, some fake push applications send out messages on a regular basis to query predetermined Web sites or servers and retrieve information (sports scores, stock quotes, news headlines). The results *appear* to be instantaneous, but behind the scenes the computer is merely polling the site, request/reply-style, over and over on a predetermined schedule. The so-called "real-time" information presented by fake push is often too old to be of value. More importantly, with fake push the network becomes even *more* congested than before, because machines are now doing the polling more frequently than people did. Everyone is still calling the time recording, but automatically, on speed dial, to find out what time it is.

There is a much better design for computerized information flow than fake push: *real* push. Publish the information out onto the network using multicast so the information is sent *just one time* when it happens, to everyone who wants it and subscribes to it. People receive only the specific information they need, network congestion is drastically reduced, and systems enjoy increased scalability. Publish/subscribe is the strategic goal of the event-driven company rendered digitally: active, intelligent, value-creating, people-seeking, platform-independent information delivered to everyone who wants it.

To manage the delivery of information, the event-driven company first designs subscription lists of news events from inside and outside the company to which each worker may subscribe for real-time updates. This copious flow is managed by sophisticated filters, which make sure that what gets to the subscriber is precisely what's needed, presented in the right order, and delivered with as much refined analysis as possible. The information is displayed on computer screens in such a way that employees are prompted—and in some cases compelled—to read it and act on it. Remember the example of the Goldman Sachs risk manager, whose computer beeped an alarm when the Warrior bought too much sterling? There's also the engineering project manager, whose computer screen blossoms with a red flag when a designer in the field changes a project specification. The engineer cannot clear the flag without taking appropriate action.

Other event-driven systems alert a sales manager when a sales rep books an order that's larger than stock on hand, an exceptional event that obliges the sales manager to either reallocate inventory from another customer or contact the sales rep to discuss the problem . . . in real time.

Subject-Based Addressing

The promise of the publish/subscribe paradigm is far richer than merely delivering the same information available via request/reply in a more timely manner and with less network congestion. Stopping there would merely be "paving the cowpath" already established by request/reply. Once information is delivered via publish/subscribe, it should begin the *keizan teian* nrichment loop, inserting itself into applications that analyze and refine it and then recirculate it, value-added, to all interested parties. But how can we identify interested parties? For that matter, how do we know who wants what information? The answer is subject-based addressing.

In 1920, Robert Sarnoff, later the founder of NBC, asked his advisors to look into the commercial potential of a new medium called radio. His people, whose minds were still attuned to the protocols of communication by telegraph, told Sarnoff radio had no future. "Who would be interested in messages addressed to nobody?" the report asked. The same disconnect prevailed in the 1980s in the emerging world of digital communications. Electronic messages within networks, such as telegrams, were (and for the most part still are) directed to specific IP addresses tied to specific users. But what if information-laden messages were addressed not to *recipients* but to the *content* of the message itself, similar to radio broadcasts. In the same way people set their radios to receive, or "subscribe" to, certain formats—classical, all-news, and so on—users on a network could set their "dials" to receive exactly what they want to know whenever a message regarding that subject is published anywhere on the network.

There's a lot more choice on the publish/subscribe network than on the standard radio dial. Some subject-based addressing systems offer subscribers 600,000 different subjects of specific information delivery. Fortunately, there are event-driven message-filtering systems up to the task of sifting out what people truly need to know. "You can't handle *all* information," writes Carla O'Dell [37] of the American Productivity and Quality Center. "Without some organizing filter . . . workers are paralyzed by information overload." This data-sifting becomes a marketable skill. One characteristic of a successful "star" employee within an event-driven company is knowing how to manage the filtering process to create the most value, acting on what's really important and letting the rest alone. The competitive advantage goes to the "star" and to the company that best walk the knife-edge between profitable chaos and worthless anarchy.

The example of a subject-addressed message I used in the previous chapter, "equities.ibm.nyse," reported the price of IBM stock. Everyone on the network who has subscribed to the price of IBM stock receives the message in real time whenever the price changes. Value is added to simple price quotations by enriching the messages' content. The "equities.ibm.nyse" message might also contain contextual and historical information, such as the price and size of the latest IBM trade, the latest bid and asked prices, and the day's volume to date of IBM trades. When that message enters a trader's workstation, the price quote itself is displayed in one part of the screen and the rest of the message's content becomes grist for analytical programs, appearing on other sections of the screen in charts and graphs showing investor trends, for example, or modeling the result of various buy-and-sell scenarios. When, seconds later, the trader acts on the original message and its freshly analyzed implications, the result is a new message reporting what has just happened. This new message is republished into the network and delivered to every person and application subscribing to developments in IBM trading, which, in turn, digest and act upon it. When does this constant enrichment cycle end? Never. It is continuous.

In enterprise applications, subject-based addressing blends data and analysis from inside and outside information sources. An excellent example is the Paging Products Group (PPG) of Motorola Corp., which uses an event-driven infrastructure to differentiate itself in a commoditized business by filling micro-customized orders with superior speed. The result equals a competitive advantage.

PPG's customers (retailers who sell pagers) want their pagers to look and feel right for kids, grandmothers, people who speak different languages, and so on. The customers therefore design and order the right product for their markets by choosing among a wide variety of options, such as display format, signal options, control button layout, alphabet, and case color. PPG's aim in linking all its order-entry, scheduling, finance, manufacturing, and shipping computer subsystems worldwide was to produce exactly what customers ordered as quickly as possible, reducing fulfillment time to as little as several hours. To achieve this, PPG/Motorola globalized the company's processes by tying together geographically disparate corporate assets into one seamless system. The new system is an active, distributed warehouse of information that Motorola can leverage to instantly and effectively respond to customer demands.

Now any retailer or Motorola sales representative can instantly receive confirmation of order fulfillment. This is possible because every factory publishes information regarding what it has available onto the network (using subject-based addressing). Orders are also published onto the network and matched with the appropriate resources at whichever factory the system determines to be the best fit (determinants could be cost, time of delivery, factory stock levels, etc.). The factories do not "poll" the system to see if new orders have come in that they can fill, nor do sales reps or computer systems have to ask individual factories whether they have the resources to fulfill an order (this would overload the system). Instead, all of Motorola's factories are tied together, creating one virtual warehouse of inventory. The consumer simply needs to say, "I'd like to buy 2,000 pagers," and they receive confirmation for when those pagers will arrive. They don't need to know which factroy to ask—such machinations are resolved by Motorola's publish/subscribe infrastructure behind the scenes.

Becoming event-driven has enabled Motorola to move from a database-centric model where constant querying of disparate systems is necessary, to an information-centric model where necessary information resources are available system wide in real time. To do this they've integrated scores of different applications running on diverse computers involving a tangle of languages, platforms, and operating systems.

The Information Bus

Depending on one's point of view, it can be said that the evolution of information technology over the past 40 years has either *enabled* or *driven* business to flatten its structure and democratize its processes to refocus on creating value for customers. It was a slow-motion revolution at first. The early, room-sized mainframes of the 1960s were mechanical doppelgängers of the hierarchical companies that installed them. Information/power was reserved for a pyramid-tip elite insulated from customer contact by layers of organizational padding. True structural business reshaping began with the minimainframe uprising of the 1970s, when individual departments within the hierarchical enterprise lost patience with the mainframe's gatekeepers and acquired their own computers. Thus (perhaps inadvertently), information technology nudged workers nearer to the concept of customer proximity, recalling Thomas Stewart's observation that, in a company where information is power, power flows toward the customer. Minimainframes liberated the flow of information, but *within departments*. Though they flattened the old management pyramid, minis validated the existence of departmental "silos"—vertical, isolated, mutually antagonistic structures.

Change accelerated after personal computers were linked into information-sharing networks. Networked PCs of the 1980s empowered entrepreneurial employees and triggered a radical pancaking of corporate structures, silos included, beginning with the drastic downsizings of the 1980s that slashed middle management. Middle management was reduced because its historic role was to act as an information-transfer layer, and that job was now being done by machines. An unintended negative consequence of middle management's demise: massive loss of accumulated institutional experience and know-how. Information technology has recently attempted to recapture and redeploy this intellectual capital via knowledge management. As discussed later, strong knowledge management is a beneficial by-product of the event-driven infrastructure.

At the time I finished graduate school and entered the high-tech sphere in the early 1980s, the structural transformations that accompanied changes from mainframe to mini to PC had brought business closer to the realization that customer value is a company's only rust-free product. But not close enough. One significant barrier remained before business could fully exploit this realization: software. Hardware had evolved toward a decentralized, distributed model, but software was still stuck in the mainframe/database era, where all information is hoarded in one location and users must know exactly where it's located and exactly how to ask for it.

Our event-driven system for financial traders was designed for a true distributed computing environment, where every machine can be a client and a server. This is known as a peer-to-peer model. The problem with traditional client/server is that it brings users no closer to data democracy. Why distinguish between passive clients that only "read" and active servers that only "publish"? Every entity on a network ought to read *and* publish. In a client/server environment, information-rich applications are assigned to particular servers, such as miniature mainframes. Once again, a person in search of information has to know which server to query. This Catch-22 quandary is inadvertently captured in Christopher Meyer's [38] *Fast Cycle Time: How to Align Purpose, Strategy, and Structure for Speed*, when Meyer wistfully says, "When available, people [in your company] can access and use knowledge if they know it exists and can find it. . . . Often, one team learns something about customer requirements that would be useful to all teams, but it never gets outside the original team." This is because the team that finds the information doesn't know where to put it so it can be found, and the team that needs the information doesn't know where to look for it or even that it exists.

This is simply not good enough! Why not tie all information sources together to create active information that goes forth to solve problems? When I first walked out into the crucible of the Goldman Sachs trading floor in 1985, I realized that Challenge No. 1 would be getting all the different data languages to speak and understand the same language. The traders, as I've mentioned, were faced with 25 different reporting sources delivered via proprietary technologies that could not communicate with one another—and were quite proud of their separateness! Fortunately, I had spent the previous year thinking in the abstract about just such a challenge. One of my earliest jobs was in hardware—designing switches, which play a key role in the presentation of information. This led me to explore the equivalent role of software. I was beginning to understand more about software and its enormous potential. As Regis McKenna [39] writes in

Real Time: Preparing for the Age of the Never-Satisfied Customer, "Software allows companies to reshape the very nature of their business. In the twenty-first century, software will be one of the most vital assets of any real-time corporation—on a par with a company's distribution system and R&D."

As a hardware guy, I'd noticed that hardware projects were designed and delivered on time as a matter of routine, but software projects were frequently late and over-budget. Considering the problem, I realized where the difference was: Hardware design projects were modularized, broken into component challenges, and parceled out to different teams. The teams worked independently on their little pieces of the puzzle and came up with solution modules. These modules were not required to communicate with other modules being designed by other teams, because when the modules were finally brought together they were all plugged into a backplane or "bus," which acted as a universal connector among the modules. Look inside any PC. There's a sort of "chassis" that the various circuit boards are plugged into. That's known as a "bus."

In precisely the same manner, though on a miniaturized scale, microchips are assembled from functional modules that are designed and built separately to solve different problems and then plugged into a bus on the chip.

Alone among the three legs of information technology, software development could not be readily modularized, because each function within the larger whole had to communicate directly with every other function. If the project were broken into pieces, the resulting solutions would have to contain complex interfaces to communicate with other solutions, which would make the project even later and even more over budget. The same need for mutual interfaces also holds when trying to integrate numbers of "complete" software programs. This requirement was responsible for the long delay in true enterprise-wide application integration.

Just as the atom, recapitulated enormously in the solar system, is a basic pattern of matter, the bus seemed to me a basic pattern of technological information transfer. There was a hardware bus and a chip bus. Why not a software bus?

For the answer I consulted a talented software colleague of mine. He said the reason I could propose a software bus in the first place was that I was "unencumbered by any detailed knowledge of software," which was essentially true. On further reflection, my colleague saw merit in the idea of a software bus, and he felt that the concept would grow in importance as distributed computing systems became more widespread. At the time I proposed the software bus, developing such a bus presented more challenges than continuing to design software the old way—that is, with connected, interfaced modules talking directly to one another. This was because in those days software, once designed, was installed on corporate systems that rarely changed configuration. But as distributed computing took hold, companies began adding new computers and servers of various types to their infrastructures, necessitating continuous reprogramming of all other computers on the network so that the old units could talk to the new additions (Figure 4.1). The idea of a software bus was becoming increasingly attractive: A software bus would allow flexible growth of distributed systems by ending the need for universal interface reprogramming every time a new node came online. New units on the bus would need to talk only to the bus in order to communicate with all other pieces on the network. In this way TIB fundamentally

Figure 4.1

Point-to-point interface vs. TIB infrastructure.

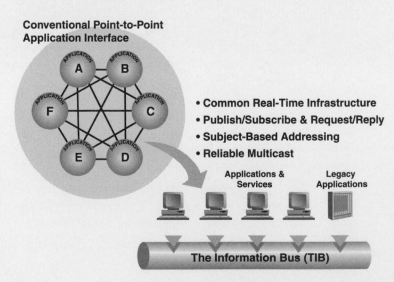

Conventional Point-to-Point Application Interface

- **Common Real-Time Infrastructure**
- **Publish/Subscribe & Request/Reply**
- **Subject-Based Addressing**
- **Reliable Multicast**

Applications & Services

Legacy Applications

The Information Bus (TIB)

simplified application integration, eliminating what many refer to as the "spaghetti" of interfaces that exist among most corporate computer systems.

What we didn't realize at the time was how extensive and varied distributed computing systems would become, incorporating mainframes, AS/400s, PCs, UNIX servers and workstations, and various networked information devices—all running on different operating systems executing complex software applications written in a bewildering variety of programming languages. The more complex and widespread distributed systems become, the more useful a universal connector such as the software bus is. (We developed and later patented this concept, which we called The Information Bus®, or TIB. Thus, my company's name: TIBCO Software Inc.)

I have described TIB as if it were a single, physical structure executing the software bus concept. In fact, technically speaking, TIB is a set of small, distributed software components that run on every machine (PC, server, etc.) connected to the network. Together, these software components create a common layer of software to which applications talk to send and receive data.

The key technical characteristics of TIB are as follows:

- A small process (also known as a daemon) runs on each node in the network and takes care of publishing data under the subject names given to it by an application. The daemon process also executes subscriptions by filtering messages on the network to select those with subject names of interest to the applications operating on its computer. The application's subscriptions are registered with the TIB daemon.

- Applications access the functionality of TIB for publishing and subscribing data via a simple application programming interface and program library.

- TIB is the software "mechanism" that brings together the key technologies of the event-driven IT architecture and includes the following capabilities:

  — Common information exchange infrastructure

  — Publish/subscribe and request/reply communications

— Subject-based addressing

— Reliable multicast for information distribution

When we first created TIB more than a decade ago, few CIOs were familiar with this type of technology, especially since the concept of distributed systems was still in its infancy. Today, CIOs and IT departments are much more familiar with messaging systems and other types of middleware—although the TIB has the additional benefit of providing the infrastructure for Internet-based business, as we'll see in more detail in Chapter 5.

Middleware and Infrastructure Software

To fully describe an event-driven IT architecture, I must take a step back and explain "middleware" and its growing role in IT. The benefits of the event-driven infrastructure—among them publish/subscribe, subject-based addressing, and messaging—are delivered via various interlocking types of middleware (of which TIB is one example). Middleware, in rather unglamorous terms, is industrial-strength plumbing that connects and integrates the complex applications and functions of computer networks, including the Internet. As its sophistication has grown, various classes of middleware have emerged to address the majority of the IT infrastructure needs of the enterprise. In more glamorous terms, middleware is akin to the old science-fiction concept of the universal translator, which allows all entities to communicate.

Middleware is defined in Claire Tristam's [40] article in *Datamation* magazine:

> Middleware lets [applications] developers avoid the issues involved in getting applications to interact with one another across multiple environments. Instead of programming transport-level instructions into each application, the programmers write extension scripts to their software to make sure their applications conform to the APIs within the middleware. The result: The foundation services underlying the APIs do all the cross-platform negotiations to make sure application requests, changes, retrievals, and updates are accomplished.

Additionally, middleware is a means of insulating applications from one another, so they don't have to be directly connected and can remain more loosely coupled.

Middleware's importance grows in proportion to the increasing complexity of distributed information technology systems. This is true inside and outside the enterprise. Linking systems within one company is challenging enough. In this age of lightning-quick mergers and acquisitions and integrated business ecosystems, where smart companies are constantly extending "outputs" and accepting "inputs" to and from other entities in their ecosystems, linking many companies' systems with many others would be downright impossible if not for middleware. Without middleware, every program in every computer in every company would require a one-to-one interface with every other program in every other computer in every other company in order to communicate. Middleware requires only that applications speak to it, not to one another.

The key demand on any middleware-based infrastructure is that it should simplify the overall technical environment. The number of "moving parts" must be reduced, or the infrastructure has not accomplished its purpose. Ironically, middleware, which was originally invented to solve confusion, has become so popular as the century draws to a close that enterprise CIOs are faced with a profusion of middleware, and some have acquired new middleware to integrate their existing middleware. In my view, this contradicts the basic principle. To be truly effective, middleware must be fully integrated and fully integrating. This does not mean that the overall infrastructure can only work with one type of middleware. However, the key is to have as seamless an environment as possible.

Middleware has grown in complexity, as have its more general technical functions, including automating the company's rule bases for work processes. Middleware now provides the facilities for companies to define the rules governing the flow of work among processes. The middleware then executes these rules as it moves data among applications. In principle, the more specifics that can be taken out of the individual applications and made generally available through the infrastructure, the more focused and simpler each individual application becomes. In other words, just as a database holds data that many applications can share, middleware can hold the process control and flow rules that many applications can use. With the expanded role and sophistication of middleware in today's IT environment, it has evolved into a complete infrastructure for connectivity, information movement, process automation, and systems management.

In 1996, as the importance of middleware was beginning to grow rapidly, the International Data Corporation (IDC) [41] issued a report about middleware's potential for use on the Internet:

> The Internet [promises] all sorts of goodness for tomorrow's business enterprise, much of it generated by increasingly distributed business applications. The technology that these [networked] business applications talk to is middleware rather than the network itself. The very essence of middleware is that this technology adds value to and shields business applications from having to communicate with the down-and-dirty details of the communications technologies that are unique to each of today's networking infrastructures. With that perspective in mind, it seems fair to forecast that the granddaddy network of all time, the Internet, looks to be the greatest stimulus ever known to drive acceptance of middleware products.

Later reports from IDC in 1999 [42] have further emphasized the importance of middleware to electronic commerce on the Internet. In fact, IDC has identified a new class of middleware known as "businessware," and defined this "as the underlying electronic commerce infrastructure for automating business processes over the Internet." The primary motivators for this technology are identified as "application integration, event-driven processing, and business process automation in a highly distributed, heterogeneous environment."

The Internet itself can even be thought of as middleware (in its most general sense), stripping away many of the idiosyncratic differences among computer languages and platforms to allow near-universal communication via the transmission control protocol/Internet protocol (TCP/IP), albeit at a primitive level. Imagine the potential both for business and consumers if the Internet were upgraded to allow reliable transmission of complex files (multimedia, business data, software upgrades, etc.) while at the same time relieving the congestion and uncertainty that now afflict the transmission of even simple files. Imagine the potential, in other words, of the Internet becoming event-driven. As I mentioned earlier in this chapter, this is exactly what is about to happen through the agency of multicasting and reliable PGM.

Reliable Multicast/PGM

I talked earlier about multicasting and PGM as ideas that would change the direction of the Internet by substituting the push of publish/subscribe for the current pull of request/reply. This change will usher in a new era: Business will finally begin to trust the Internet for scalable broadcast of its critical information. Fortunately, this acceptance of the Internet by business will not create even more congestion problems than we have today, because multicast, in addition to being reliable and scalable, is bandwidth-friendly. Internet multicasting, or IP Multicast, is to TCP/IP as radio broadcasting is to one-to-one telephone connections, with one major difference. As with a radio station, multicast broadcasts messages just once, and streaming networking technology then delivers that message to as many "listeners" as are tuned in. If the "message" is a software upgrade, for example, IP Multicast will broadcast it to the 300,000 people registered to receive the upgrade by putting it out over the Internet just once. In the current request/reply model, all 300,000 people would have to visit the software company's Web site to request the upgrade. Then the Web site would have to send the upgrade over the Internet 300,000 times. Multicast is far more democratic than radio. It requires no license to multicast on the Internet. Nor does it require expensive or powerful "transmission" equipment. Any multicaster, no matter how limited his or her bandwidth connection to the Internet, can reach a potentially unlimited audience.

The concept of multicasting emerged in the early 1980s, and a few years later provided a congestion solution for our team during the refinement of the first publish/subscribe systems for financial institutions. Similar to the Internet, those first systems were point-to-point, unicasting systems that did not scale. Multicasting was the best cure for this, but it was not yet reliable enough. In trading situations, reliability has to be perfect. Simple multicasting creates a message stream. If you're streaming voice or video and a bit of the message gets lost, there might be a momentary hitch in the voice or one pixel on the screen might black out for a moment. (Additionally, there's software that can read the problem and smooth it out before it's audible or visible.) But when you're streaming business information, a little loss of signal can equal a big loss of money, and there's no software that can guess what the real numbers ought to be. A customer can order 500 shares of stock and it comes through as "50" or "unknown," and that's trouble. So we added "negative acknowledgment," which allows the message destination to notice something is missing and request a retransmission from the sending end. This trustworthy form is called "reliable" multicast.

The same pattern, echoed, is at work today on the Internet. People who use the Internet have been as excited about the capabilities of the Internet as the financial traders were about the early publish/subscribe systems. As with the traders, Internet users have come close to bringing the unicasting system to its knees with their excited usage. The next step is bandwidth-conserving multicast. Most of the major Internet companies have now come to accept the potentials of IP Multicast. The only alternative is to do what WorldCom COO John Sidgmore told the *San Francisco Chronicle* [43] his firm was doing: "Build networks 1,000 times larger. And do it every six months or so."

The point of PGM on the Internet, as with reliable multicast on intranets before it, is to make network multicasting sufficiently trustworthy for companies to send business-critical messages streaming across the Internet using the publish/subscribe paradigm. Similar to reliable multicast, PGM contains "negative acknowledgment" components that will notice the absence of any part of the message and ask the broadcaster to retransmit a whole message. This development will extend the benefits of becoming an event-driven company to many more organizations.

Some large enterprises have long had the wherewithal to create worldwide private networks to link their operations into an event-driven infrastructure while avoiding the problems of the Internet. Now organizations with even modest resources can adopt event-driven information flow and enjoy the same benefits as the richest companies, because the Internet is evolving into a similarly robust, worldwide wide area network (WAN). And similarly, companies equipped with ample resources can opt to take advantage of the ubiquity of the Internet now that reliable and efficient methods of information distribution are available.

How NASDAQ Is Using Multicasting

Here's one example of how a large institution is relying on multicasting and real-time infrastructure software to develop next-generation information distribution systems. The NASDAQ Stock Market, which operates the world's largest electronic trading floor, is standardizing on real-time middleware to distribute digital information in the fastest and most efficient manner possible and to strengthen its entire digital infrastructure. The new NASDAQ digital infrastructure is expected to become the model for financial institutions that send real-time market data to professional traders and individual investors via the Internet.

Network traffic from NASDAQ computers will be significantly reduced by being able to broadcast a single message, or stock price, that instantaneously makes its way through the network to millions of users, rather than having to send a million individual messages to millions of users. In addition, network users will be able to have customized information sent to them, automatically, instead of having to query computer databases.

Currently, NASDAQ trades over 700 million shares a day and was the first stock market to handle over 1 billion shares on a single day. By standardizing on middleware and leveraging multicasting's bandwidth-conserving capabilities, NASDAQ will be able to handle dramatic increases in share volume (up to 8 billion shares a day).

NASDAQ sets the standard for growth, technical leadership, and innovation in its industry. It is also the quintessential event-driven enterprise, where everyone must share information at the same time, in real time. By using event-driven technology, NASDAQ and its technology partners have built what is arguably the world's most advanced stock market.

Event-Driven Technology Infrastructure

The event-driven IT architecture consists of six key, integrated components or layers (Figure 4.2). Together, these six components provide a complete IT infrastructure for moving, managing, and integrating information:

1. **Messaging**—The fundamental layer of the event-driven architecture, the messaging component, is TIB (or something TIB-like). This layer is the transport for all information exchanged among applications. The messaging layer provides a variety of communications models, including request/reply, but leverages publish/subscribe for maximum efficiency in the distribution of information. This component must be able to reliably and rapidly move information where it needs to go. Subject-based addressing is the naming scheme used to tag and route information. Additionally, it is critical that the messaging system support a variety of "information devices," not just PCs. This is especially important with the accelerating use of wireless communications.

2. **Adapters**—This component consists of the software needed to connect applications not originally designed for the messaging system in use. If an application is built with the messaging system in mind, an adapter is not necessary. Adapters are necessary in the cases of legacy,

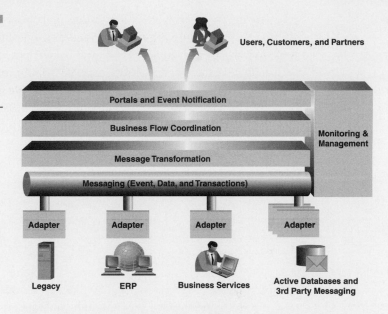

Figure 4.2
Event-driven
IT infra-
structure
components.

custom-built, or third-party applications to convert the APIs, protocols, and data types of the external applications to compatibility with the messaging environment. The adapters ensure that the external application behaves as if it were native to the messaging environment in use. This component is also used to connect to other middleware environments. Though simplicity is middleware's raison d'être, most large companies today have more than one infrastructure technology, and the need exists to integrate them. This layer ensures transparent linkage between the environments.

3. Message transformation—This component works with or without an adapter to provide general message transformation capabilities; that is, it transforms the content and syntax of a message from one predefined format into another. This is used to take a message from one system and convert it into a structure that can be consumed by another. Message transformation is a critical component in an environment with a diverse set of applications.

4. Business flow coordination—This component governs how various types of information flow among processes.

It automates business process execution across applications, coordinating the logic that exists within each application. This ensures coherent business process execution at the enterprise level. Because this component automates the overall business logic of the enterprise, it prevents having to repeat this logic within each application or each point-to-point interface between applications (as would be the case without middleware).

5. Portals and event notification—To take full advantage of the content flowing through the infrastructure, general-purpose tools exist to allow people to tap into the information sources of the enterprise, much as a financial trader taps into market information and news. Exciting visualizations can help engage a worker's imagination. Some variants under development include "flying" through a 3-D virtual reality landscape, where representative elements are used for sales-results tables and other statistical materials. The corporate portal is a useful visualization tool for delivering content to employees, partners, or customers in a customizable format. The corporate portal represents such an important facet of the event-driven IT infrastructure that I have devoted Chapter 5 to it.

6. Monitoring and management—Distributed systems mean more machines and a more complicated systems administration problem. This problem can be addressed through automation. An event-driven architecture distributes information about internal system events as well as external business events and can thereby track notifications of problems within the environment. Management systems deploy rule bases to each machine in the network so that when typical problems occur, the local management software can take self-corrective action. This technology is not science fiction. It is one of the fastest growing segments of the technology marketplace and holds out the promise of operating extensive IT infrastructures with less than an army of system administrators. Additionally, this component encompasses general

security facilities, and the mechanisms to administer and control what subjects are established and who can publish to them and subscribe to them.

Together, these pieces provide a complete set of services for moving, managing, and integrating information in the event-driven enterprise. An enterprise can take limited advantage of this architecture by using only a few of the components (say, messaging only), but the maximum benefits accrue when all the components exist as an integrated set.

Simplifying Application Integration

Let's apply the event-driven architecture to a typical set of enterprise applications (Figure 4.3). In a conventional client/server environment, "client" applications have fixed connections to "server" applications. Point-to-point, "spaghetti" interfaces abound. These interfaces represent a complex set of dependencies among the applications. Remove one interface and the ripple effect through the overall architecture can be significant. In addition, the information used by the applications is isolated into separate databases, which are connected only to

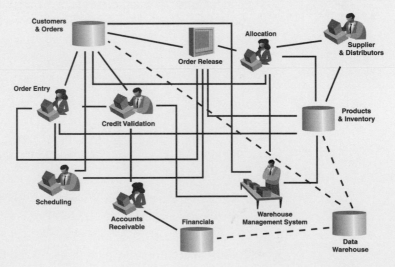

Figure 4.3

The contemporary organization.

specific sets of applications. Information remains passive—not moving until asked for. The cost of change in this environment is high, especially as the number and complexity of systems grow.

The solution is to eliminate the spaghetti of interfaces among applications with a set of middleware components—the event-driven IT infrastructure—that handle all the application integration and information exchange requirements. In the event-driven approach, applications have only one interface (to the middleware) instead of to each other. The databases now become part of the overall integrated architecture, accessible to any authorized application. Information can now be moved automatically through the infrastructure, creating a virtual river of information. Instead of information linkages restricting flexibility, the flow of information now allows applications (or even machines) to change location, new applications to be added, and old applications removed, without affecting the overall IT architecture. The infrastructure insulates against the negative impacts of change, allowing the organization to easily adapt to changing needs and conditions.

The key differences between event-driven and older information distribution paradigms include the following:

■ Event-driven information moves in the form of "messages" generated by business events, instead of through requests for updates. Content distribution is in real time and is automatic.

■ Adapters and message transformation facilities convert all message types into universally consumable content.

■ Subjects (not addresses) are used to tag and categorize information. If an application, or user, needs different content, the application or the user can expand the subscription list (rather than change its interface), dramatically reducing the programming effort required.

■ Business rules defined within the infrastructure route content via subjects based on detected conditions in the information or the process flow.

■ Because incoming transactions or events are captured and distributed simultaneously to all relevant applications for processing, business process cycles are compressed through the parallelization of activities. Applications processing events generate further events, as needed, which are also blasted out through the infrastructure, enabling a high "fan out" of processing activities.

■ Visualization applications allow people to dynamically tune into different content sources via subjects. Users receive alerts and special bulletins by subjects. Generally, the user is able to customize his or her display to reflect individual information requirements, from receiving e-mails to displaying prominent alerts on the monitor screen, or through the use of a portal.

■ Exceptions—situations that require human intervention—are published under special subjects or identified by specific content and are pushed up from the infrastructure into the relevant applications and onto the desktops of those who need to take appropriate action.

■ As internal staff can, customers can also use visualization capabilities such as portals to tap into whatever finely segmented information they choose to explore, leading to highly focused, real-time interactions with customers.

Bechtel's event-driven system offers an excellent technical inside view of an event-driven IT architecture (Figure 4.4). This

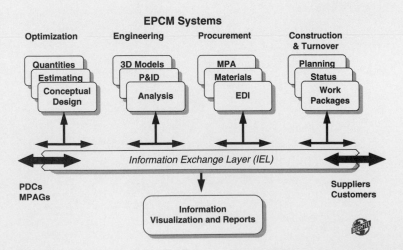

Figure 4.4

Bechtel's IEL infrastructure.

architecture provides a common set of services and facilities to ensure that the hundreds of applications involved in engineering, procurement, construction, and management worldwide can exchange information on an event-driven basis. In addition, this infrastructure is accessible to authorized suppliers and joint venture partners, allowing the flexible exchange of real-time information with the systems of these other companies. Bechtel refers to the basic middleware infrastructure as "the IEL" (or Information Exchange Layer). The IEL handles all the messaging, message transformation, caching, adaptation of external applications, and subject administration.

Enabling Content Integration

The event-driven IT architecture is a hub that integrates and circulates content among applications. As shown in Figure 4.5, the typical enterprise deals with content that exists in a variety of forms and in a variety of application technologies, such as custom-built applications, purchased systems (a financial accounting or manufacturing system), e-mail, desktop tools (Word or PowerPoint), real-time data feeds, and various types of databas-

Figure 4.5

The event-driven enterprise.

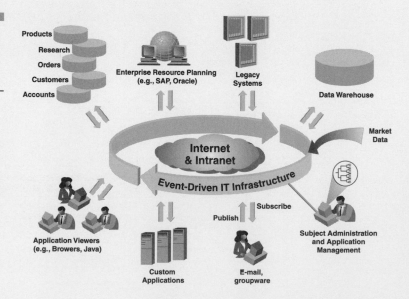

es (including data warehouses). Translating content among systems for general use through the IT infrastructure is nearly impossible with client/server technology.

Similar to the traders I first encountered on the Goldman Sachs trading floor, who were trying to assemble information from an array of incommunicado monitors, workers in client/server-based companies end up juggling a variety of technologies, each for accessing some particular kind of information. These workers waste time and effort uselessly moving information between incompatible technologies. A simple example is the time wasted in some banking environments translating front-office data into a language back-office applications can understand. Why not simply tie all systems together via the event-driven architecture? Many of the world's largest banks are in the process of doing just that.

The event-driven approach to integration, as shown in Figure 4.6, uses middleware to provide a common publish/subscribe exchange mechanism for information and to "normalize" the various types of content (such as Bechtel's IEL). The components of the architecture transform and translate information from one form to another to allow content sharing across application technologies. The infrastructure creates a continuously active flow between business processes.

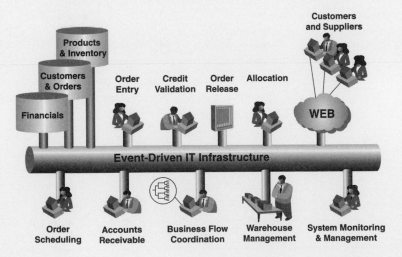

Figure 4.6

The event-driven IT infrastructure.

Nomura's Event-Driven IT Infrastructure

Another good example of using event-driven technology to integrate applications and information for competitive advantage is Nomura, an international bank with its head office in London, England. Life at Nomura before Geoff Doubleday, Managing Director of IT, and his team arrived was rather low-tech. Mainframe back-office systems were inflexible and offered limited access to either information or desktop productivity tools. Trading systems were bought piecemeal for different departments. Consequently, the team's job was to provide the business with a technology platform for the next century, upon which a new generation of business applications could be layered.

Nomura's senior management had the foresight to recognize that their three-year, £40-million technology investment would be the firm's most important competitive weapon, after the quality of its personnel.

Today over 30 percent of Nomura's revenue is generated internationally. This revenue is composed of a variety of products and services that reflect Nomura's increasingly diverse, global operations. As a result, Nomura Securities stands shoulder to shoulder with the leading global securities firms from the United States and Europe.

Despite this progress, Nomura was keen to seek new advantage through the radical use of IT. This meant not just looking at new technologies but also questioning accepted wisdom about current IT strategies. They particularly looked in detail at the model of client/server computing and considered new components that could optimize the use of a client/server architecture within the demanding business environment operating in the financial markets.

Nomura's strategy is based on a three-tier client/server architecture. The top layer is the desktop graphical user interface (GUI); layer two is the business application's servers; and layer three is composed of database servers, resources servers, and communications gateways. Critically, these layers sit above an enterprise-wide information distribution platform. It's the role of this platform that is essential to the success of the overall architecture.

This strategy led Nomura to adopt The Information Bus (TIB) platform across all of Nomura's operations, far beyond the front office, to add new functionality and manage the demands of enterprise-wide transaction processing. Doubleday's team recognized that, when applied across the enterprise, publish/subscribe and subject-based addressing could provide many of the processing and communications characteristics vital to make the Nomura architecture a reality. Without the application integration architecture provided by TIB, the potential value of everything sitting above the platform would be compromised.

The Information Bus platform distributes—or "publishes"— information across the network in a consistent format. The data are "self-describing." This means that individual business applications in the front, middle, or back office receive—or "subscribe" to—only those pieces of information required for that specific application, be it transaction data or market price information.

Publish/subscribe technologies allow applications to share real-time information seamlessly with other applications on the network, regardless of location, platform, or type of application. Information producers publish information without needing to know how it will be used; while information consumers subscribe to available information without needing to know where it comes from.

This decoupling of producers and consumers is the breakthrough in client/server communications that Nomura sought. The benefits are found in easier application development, maintenance, and operation. Because the information is mission critical, TIB platform's guaranteed delivery and store-and-forward features ensure transaction data can't be "lost" among different applications.

The advantages to Nomura of the new architecture can be measured in many different ways. Using front-end market data display software, traders can access any TIB distributed information, including real-time market data, internal information, news, video, and graphs, as well as information from other applications. To make it easy for traders the same naming conventions are used, regardless of the nature or location of the information source.

Aside from giving traders an information edge, Nomura expects, eventually, to save up to £2 million per year just from the flexibility to move individuals more easily within the organization. Up to 50 people are relocated within the company every weekend. Now any individual can access the information and business applications he or she needs from any desktop, eliminating this logistical support headache. Furthermore, users can do this through a single workstation, rather than using multiple terminals.

Whereas the typical securities operation has built its technology infrastructure around the requirements of two distinct front- and back-office departments, Nomura established the view that the role of the middle office was at the center of its information distribution architecture.

This means that data are stored once only, within the middle office, and then published to the front office for position-keeping and to the back office for accounting. This database retains both static and moving (i.e., real-time) data—the former being information about counterparties, clients, standard settlement instructions, and so on, and the latter being trading and market price information.

As a result, all areas of the firm use consistent data. This eliminates the arguments about reconciliation that are common to most trading operations (if front, middle, and back offices each maintain a separate P&L, invariably none of them reconcile).

Consistency is also a benefit in other ways. One server maintains a single library of the different models for calculating prices and values used across the whole organization. Normally these are developed by different trading desks or departments and amended locally. Maintaining common models, algorithms, and methodologies ensures that senior managers can have confidence in the quality of information gathered for P&L and reporting purposes.

Desktop clients are a 50/50 mix of Compaq PCs and Sun workstations; all the servers are Sun open systems; and clients and servers are linked via a single TCP/IP network. In total this represents some 1,200 clients and 400 servers. The system has been applied not just in London but also in Nomura's offices in Paris, Frankfurt, Zurich, Milan, Amsterdam, Geneva, Lugano, and Luxembourg.

The scale of the overall project is huge and, while cost savings have been identified as a result, for Doubleday justification is not sought in terms of cost reduction: "The project is justified by the commercial advantage in being able to do things better. The infrastructure, and the tools we can use as a result of having the infrastructure, means that the development should pay for itself in two to three years."

Managing Subjects

When I describe the event-driven architecture to people, one of the most common questions they ask is, "How is the set of subjects to which each worker or application subscribes managed and maintained?" The answer is, "With some effort." In my experience, the level of control of subjects varies among organizations and among situations within the same organization. The first step is to establish an initial subject map, in much the same way developers create a database design before implementing a database. Unlike a database, however, the structure of subjects is more fluid and tends to change more frequently over time. The initial subject map is needed to get the overall architecture started, so application designers know what subjects are already defined. The screen shot depicted in Figure 4.7 illustrates how one organization has equipped employees to access subject lists and to select which data to subscribe to. The subjects are organized hierarchically, much like Windows organizes files in a system of trees-trees of folders, subfolders, and files within folders.

Creating a map of your organization's subjects is not a trivial task, and it takes serious thought. The structure or map of your subjects needs to be based on the fundamental types of information used by the organization. In this sense, subject name mapping is a little like mapping (or modeling) data for database design. The key difference is that subjects represent a much

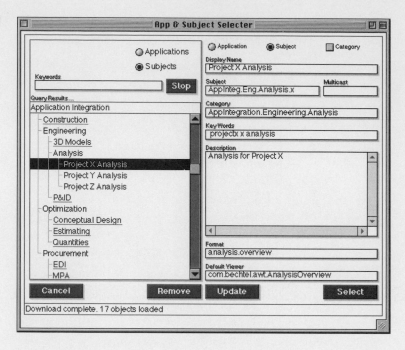

more flexible and dynamically extendable definition of information. There are no optimization or complex technical design requirements for subject name mapping (as there are for database design). All of the subject names are registered in a directory (as shown in Figure 4.7). This directory and the tools used to query and update it form the means by which an organization's subjects are administered and managed, including individual user permission for accessing certain subjects. The directory can be queried to find existing subjects, or new subjects as they are added. However, because push is always more informative than pull, people can be notified of new subjects by subscribing to a subject established specifically for the purpose of announcing new subject names.

The subject directory can be described as follows:

■ It retains a single definition of what each subject means throughout the organization.

■ It defines permissions regarding who can access which subjects.

■ It provides a single point of control for establishing new subjects.

Once a set of subjects is established, the organization must decide how strictly the various subject categories need to be controlled. As with all corporate information, there are limits to who should look at certain information. Personnel data, for example, are not data that should be published on a globally accessible subject basis. Conversely, relevant news from inside and outside the company should be as widely available as possible throughout the organization. Ultimately, management decides which subjects are confidential and/or not appropriate for large-scale access.

It is important to note that being event-driven does not mean that everyone in the company has to receive reports on every subject. People subscribe (or are subscribed) to the subjects they need to do their jobs. These subjects may change over time or even change through the course of the day. To access available subjects, users consult an electronic directory of subjects, or they receive notification of a new subject. Based on the user's individual permissions, subjects can be selected for publishing or subscribing. When applications are developed or installed, they are similarly configured and given permission to use certain subjects. The environment allows the subjects used to change for individuals and applications, according to preestablished permissions.

The management process by which permissions are set is similar to the process by which most organizations set up user network accounts. Restricted subjects require management approval for access, which, once granted, is put into effect through a subject "administrator" (similar to a system administrator) employing the appropriate tools. In some cases, a manager can grant access using the tool directly. The event-driven structure is used to best advantage when it remains easy for people to access available subjects, be notified of new ones, and establish new ones to meet the changing needs of the organization.

Every company's culture will dictate the degree to which information flows freely. My advice is always to let the information flow as freely and as openly as possible. As we are about to see, one of the event-driven company's greatest strengths is its ability to exploit open systems to its advantage. Systems within the company, therefore, ought to be wide open as well. I have rarely seen situations where a company faltered because its workers were given too much information, but I have often seen situations where a company faltered because its workers were given too little information.

Management by Exception

A company that becomes event-driven can change shape radically as its structure conforms to its new business logic. One dramatic example is Luxembourg-based Cedel Bank. Founded in 1970 to clear and settle trades in Eurobonds, Cedel has since grown to become a global settlement business, encompassing all varieties of bonds, securities, and exchanges. Becoming event-driven reduced the time it took Cedel Bank to clear trades between securities buyers and sellers (giving the buyer his or her securities, giving the seller his or her money) from seven days to real time, and it concomitantly changed Cedel's management structure from a decorous, 41-member board that met in Luxembourg, to front-line account executives situated where the customers are located: regional offices in London, New York, Tokyo, and Hong Kong.

As an event-driven company, Cedel Bank now "manages by exception," automating routine tasks—in its case, routine processing of settlement instructions—so people can exploit the rich opportunities to be mined from exceptions. Management by exception means that Cedel can settle more trades more quickly, because routine processing is fully automated. Wherever possible, trades proceed directly from initial capture through all intermediate steps to final settlement without manual intervention. This is referred to as "straight-through processing," since nothing stops the trade from beginning to end— all aspects of the process work together automatically. This means that Cedel's customers have their money "tied-up" for less time waiting for transactions to clear and settle. Putting money in the customer's pocket is one sure way to ensure a competitive advantage. In addition, Cedel can focus on offering its customers more services, such as special financing to accommodate exceptional circumstances where the customer has insufficient funds to settle the trade.

Management by exception attempts to expand upon the "80/20 rule" that many of us see on a daily basis. This rule states that 80 percent of the value of most tasks is achieved in the first 20 percent of the effort. Conversely, the last 20 percent of value ends up taking the lion's share of the effort (or 80 percent). Companies and many individuals try to optimize their work with the 80/20 rule in mind, by trying to stay focused on delivering the bulk of the value in any task and avoiding or limiting effort on the energy-wasting last 20 percent of the value. This is really another way of remaining conscious of the point of diminishing returns in any activity. So, the 80/20 rule describes typical workflow in a non-event-driven company: Focus on balancing efforts to ensure that the most value is delivered for the least investment of time and effort. Unfortunately, this approach can tend to focus people on the optimization of routine tasks, which ultimately shortchanges the customer, because the goal becomes achieving just-good-enough rewards with minimal effort. This works, at least for a while, but it also has the side effect of wasting human time on tasks a machine could more easily handle. This is commodity thinking.

The event-driven goal is more extreme: Devote 100 percent of the company's human resources to exceptions, 0 percent to routine. At this moment such a goal may seem just out of reach, but it is not far off. The focus now becomes twofold: achieving best efficiency from routine efforts through automation, while enabling maximum business leverage to be gained from the exceptional events. Everyone becomes focused on creating new opportunities, rather than optimizing the known ones.

Even the most successful financial traders are not completely invulnerable to automation. The CIO of a large European bank recently told me he believes that many of his astronomically compensated traders eventually will be replaced with event-driven automation, leaving just a few humans (compensated at multiple astronomical levels) to handle the most exceptional opportunities. Whatever your product or service, the closer your company comes to managing totally by exception, the better it is deploying its workforce and the more value it is creating for its customers, its workers, and itself.

In practice, management by exception is relatively simple, although it may be technically difficult to implement. Basically, management by exception relies on someone or some computer system to sift through the mass of routine information and events to identify those that fall outside of normal operating parameters. A simple example is identifying a customer order requiring special handling—such as a unique product configuration or extraordinary credit terms. The order becomes important not only because it needs management approval to proceed (e.g., extending credit to the customer), but because it says something about the customer and the market that may be useful in shaping the company's business strategy.

A more complex example is where the exceptions start to become more frequent—the odd orders start to become near normal. The fact that you know of the exceptions immediately is important, because you can respond rapidly to the market changes they might imply. But what is more important is that you are *focused* on the exceptions. To understand this fully, think of how many opportunities are missed simply because someone is too busy with "work," often routine work, to realize the potential of an opportunity (or a problem) and act on it. Management by exception forces the company to focus on the opportunities and the problems so that their significance can be seen more clearly.

In a sense, management by exception is not really new—it's what many managers (particularly executive managers) strive for. They only want to deal with the significant or unusual—those events for which the executive's experience and time can be best leveraged. Traditionally, the executive relied on clerks and on middle management to sift through information, compiling reports and analyzing data for exceptional conditions and emerging trends. But the "right-sizing" efforts of the 1980s reduced the resources available for sifting through information and performing the analysis.

Technology became the answer, and corporations looked to it to replace middle management. Technology can, of course, perform the routine processing well and identify exceptional items for management review. However, the removal of people and insufficient technological capabilities to automate human judgment have left *too many* exceptions for many managers in the right-sized world of the 1990s.

Two key elements need to be in place for technology to bridge the gap. First, the knowledge of what is exceptional must be captured and accurately automated (not easy, especially if sophisticated exception identification is required). If the knowledge automated is too basic, too many exceptions result. The more sophisticated the automation, the more effective management by exception can be. Second, the automated processes must have access to *all* the data necessary to determine what constitutes an exception. Without real-time information, management by exception is of limited benefit.

Ideally, as business events occur, they are pushed out into an event-driven IT environment, where they are monitored in real time by systems that embody the necessary exception identification logic through a system of rules. Events that pass (or fail—depending on your perspective) the exception criteria are forwarded to applications viewed by the relevant person (not always a manager), as shown in Figure 4.8. Overall, the person handling the exceptions sees only the exceptions, to which he or she can devote every effort to assessing and acting upon them.

One example of management by exception that we have already discussed is the financial trader, whose MarketSheet alerts him or her to potentially profitable developments. Another example can be found in high-tech manufacturing enterprises, such as consumer electronics companies. In several such companies, all steps in the order-entry, production-planning/scheduling, and warehousing/production/distribution processes are completely managed by exception. Integrated computers and applications systems handle all conventional orders. When the systems detect an exception—orders for customized prod-

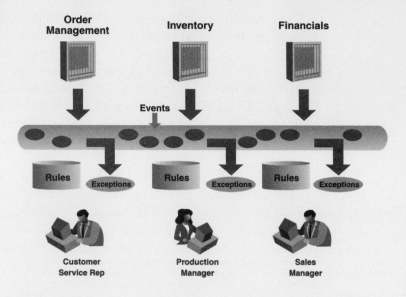

uct features that necessitate product or process invention, large orders that require extra capital outlay for raw materials, questionable customer credit, a request for expedited delivery—human intervention is immediately summoned.

Significantly, the people who are summoned to deal with exceptions are, in most cases, not managers but those in closest contact with the customers. Sales people are actually empowered to modify the factories' workflows if the sales reps think such intervention will boost customer value. The event-driven company thus makes enormous power available to employee "stars," regardless of their apparent rank.

The most wisely used event-driven infrastructure will blend germane news developments from inside and outside the company. There should, in fact, be little differentiation of "inside" and "outside." The financial world, the first business ecosystem to become event-driven, has no such dichotomy: News events in the "outside world" have enormous impact on the "inside world." As suggested in a February 1998 speech by Peter Drucker [44], leaders in all business ecosystems should insist that their workers keep track of what's happening outside the walls. "The biggest single challenge you face is to organize outside data, because change occurs from the outside," Drucker told the Fortune IT Strategy Forum in Pebble Beach, California. "Management is swamped with inside data but doesn't have any more real information than it did 40 years ago, and the quality of decisions has not improved." In a true ecosystem there are no walls. No inside. No outside. Everything affects everything else.

CHAPTER 5

event-driven.com

Make the Internet Work for You

The Internet is probably the most significant force in the history of information technology. It has had a dramatic impact on our lives and the way we do business, and it represents a massive opportunity for commercial enterprises. So now that I've agreed with what every other technology pundit says, let me also suggest that the Internet *alone* isn't sufficient to dramatically improve your business performance. A myth has developed around what it means to conduct "e-business" and become an "e-corporation": create a Web site, let it process transactions, and new business will simply fly in the door. Nothing could be further from the truth. If you have a slow, inefficient, and insufficient service that you offer over the telephone and you begin to offer that same service over the Internet, you still have a slow, inefficient, and insufficient service—except now your customers can become unsatisfied over the Web instead of the telephone. This is another version of paving cowpaths. People have the right sense of the problem—in wanting to solve it by adding the "e" to their business—and the right impression that something dramatic needs to change, but if you think of e-business as the Internet alone, you're headed down the wrong path.

The key to successful use of the Internet is to see it as an extension, rather than an appendage, of your event-driven enterprise. The best way to do this is to create a comprehensive, dynamic platform for the content and services of your company that is more than a Web site. This is called a "portal" and provides an easy way for customers to access your products and services over the Internet. The portal is more than a Web site, because it is active, tying together multiple processes, information sources, and systems under one point of access and one graphically rich display. This is how the visionary companies of the next millennium will exploit the Internet.

Embracing the Internet is probably inevitable for virtually any business. The Internet alone will not make your business competitive, because an Internet sales channel isn't necessarily inexpensive and isn't automatically more profitable. This is what the outdoor gear and apparel company Recreational Equipment Inc. (REI) discovered when it created its Internet-based sales channel, rei.com. REI has found rei.com to be an expensive and difficult undertaking, although still worthwhile [45]. It has invested significant time and money in its Internet-based business and believes that it will continue to be a costly sales channel to maintain. The point is that you have to be prepared to invest significant effort to make the Internet work for your business—it isn't automatically cheaper or more efficient.

The editors of *Fortune Magazine* [46] recently defined the e-corporation as follows:

> As the term suggests, a real E-corporation isn't just using the Internet to alter its approach to markets and customers; it's combining computers, the Web, and the massively complex programs known as enterprise software to change everything about how it operates.

I like this definition because it is holistic. Changing "everything about how it operates" means, as the *Fortune* definition suggests, leveraging all the IT assets of your enterprise, including, and most importantly I would contend, its core business systems. If your core business systems aren't tied directly to your Internet-based sales channels, one of two things has occurred:

1. You've created systems specifically for your Internet channel that are duplicate systems, which you now have to integrate with your core business systems.

2. Incoming Internet transactions are being manually processed from your Web site into your core business systems (i.e., your back office), creating duplicate manual processing.

Either way, you may have gained something from the Internet, but you've diminished your gains by creating other inefficiencies. You've missed the really big opportunity to create a seamless electronic infrastructure that stretches from your back office to your front office and out over the Internet, which is exactly what an event-driven infrastructure allows you to do.

I would add to the *Fortune* definition, that a key benefit of the combination of Internet and mobile information devices is the ability to service customers "anytime, anywhere." The event-driven company may be highly responsive inside its own walls, but the Internet allows it to extend the reach and scope of customers and business partners that can be incorporated into its flow of events. Embracing the Internet after becoming event-driven (rather than instead of) makes sense, because you then have something good (or something better) to offer, as well as the means in place to rapidly capitalize on the opportunities the Internet provides.

Two or three years from now, every company will be using the Internet in some way. But if you make your business event-driven and present it to the outside world through the mechanism of a portal, you have become an e-corporation, because you will have made the core IT changes needed to take maximum advantage of your business potential in an Internet context.

Extend Your Business with a Portal

You are probably already using a portal when you surf the Web, even though you might not know it under that label. Yahoo!, for example, is one of the first and largest commercial portals. In its simplest terms, a portal is a gateway to a collection of information and services; it simplifies the means by which you find and access information and online services by providing a single organizational scheme and single access point. In the case of Yahoo! or AOL/Netscape's Netcenter, the portal is literally a gateway into the Internet itself.

More precise definitions of portals distinguish them from mere Web sites by highlighting the aggregation and organizational capabilities that a portal provides. Early portal implementations (such as Yahoo! in its early days) were really only search engines or taxonomies for Web sites. Today, portals such as Yahoo! have evolved to include a more sophisticated organizational model for making sense of large amounts of information, as well as providing access to shopping, auctioning, chat, and other services. A Web site provides some organized information, but a portal provides the integration and organization of many more types of content and services, including linkages to other sites. The underlying value of the portal is that it provides two key elements:

1. A single access point to multiple content sources and services.

2. A coherent, structured method for organizing the content sources and services available.

In this way, a portal is more than just a collection of linkages and more than a search engine, because it provides an easy (or at least, easier) way to navigate and use the information and services available. As portals evolve, they are offering a broader range of capabilities. As with an event-driven organization, they are becoming more dynamic and more personalized. Yahoo! and Netcenter both provide personalization capabilities (My Yahoo and My Netcenter, respectively) that allow you to create a customized view of what you're interested in. As these portals become more sophisticated, they will constantly update and reorganize themselves to provide the user with the optimal view of what's available.

The value that a portal can bring, and the value that it can represent, is evidenced by the multibillion dollar market values of the major portals: Yahoo! at about $34 billion and Lycos at over $4.7 billion (as of July 1999). These valuations are comparable to the valuations of the content providers themselves, such as Reuters at approximately $19 billion and Dow Jones at just under $4 billion. Remember that the Internet portal companies have reached these massive valuations from the public markets without creating any real content. They are organizing access to other companies' content. Certainly much of the value of the top players comes from the brand names they have created. But even this points out what I believe is critical to a successful portal: the ability to create a unique experience. It may seem obvious, but the brand is only valuable when it can be attached to something meaningful and unique to the customer.

Portals are not just useful for organizing the content and services of the Internet for the Internet public at large (as is the case with Yahoo!, Netscape, Lycos, AltaVista, etc.). Portals also serve as a valuable method for corporations or organizations to present content and services to a segmented or select group of Internet or intranet users. In an enterprise context, a portal is often used to aggregate and organize the content and services of that particular enterprise for use by its employees, customers, and business partners. In this situation, a portal is referred to as an enterprise information portal (EIP), a corporate portal or a vertical portal. The definition often gets a bit fuzzy, because an elaborate corporate Web site might be—wrongly—christened an EIP. An EIP is different from a Web site, because it provides a unifying infrastructure for multiple services *and* content. Another important distinction is that the EIP provides the infrastructure for a much more active and personalized interaction with the user than a typical Web site.

Let me explain. When based on an event-driven IT infrastructure, an EIP is uniquely enabled to deliver active, personalized content. The basic publish/subscribe and subject-based addressing capabilities of the event-driven IT infrastructure allow EIP users to select and receive exactly the information desired, in much the same way as employees inside the event-driven enterprise receive information. In addition, the same types of management facilities are available to control which people can access which types of content and services. Without event-driven technology, the EIP can't be comprehensive enough or dynamic enough to respond to changing market requirements and offer new or modified services and content. A more brittle implementation approach to connect your business systems directly to your EIP with point-to-point interfaces would require having to virtually rebuild your EIP every time you need to add a new system, content source, or service—not a very practical situation if you're trying to operate at Internet speed.

Another variation of the EIP is specialized commercial portals that fit specific market niches. This type of portal is meant to cater to special interests within the Internet community and may even be transient, forming for special events, such as the Olympics, and dissolving after the event is over. An example of this type of portal is CBS Sportsline. CBS Sportsline is a public portal site for sports enthusiasts, who want their sports news in real time. At www.sportsline.com, sports fans can get up-to-the-second information on all kinds of sporting events, access information on their favorite teams/players (bios, news, etc.), and purchase tickets and sporting memorabilia. Although these types of portals are still evolving, their purpose is to offer more detail about topic areas than a Yahoo! will want to offer. Portals such as Yahoo! will become the superportal, directing you to the next layer of specialized portals that will provide a highly granular set of information and services.

For the same reasons that the major commercial portals are highly valued—aggregation and organization of content and ease of use—EIPs will be of great value to individual companies. Christmas 1998 showed the power of Internet commerce, with a dramatic upturn in online shopping. The value of online transactions went up 230 percent from 1997 [47]. This dramatic increase appears to make 1998 the watershed year for electronic commerce on the Internet. However, the one criticism that seemed universal following Christmas 1998 was that using the Internet for shopping still wasn't as easy as it should be. The achievement of even higher transaction rates and faster growth rates will depend on making the access to commerce services simpler. The demand for online shopping appears to exist, but use will be accelerated by portal technology, which will make it easier and faster for shoppers to find and buy what they want. The battle for eyeballs is on. Are you ready to win them?

How Sticky Is Your Portal?

The world of portals involves a new lexicon. From this lexicon you need to be aware of three key terms that impact the effectiveness of any portal, whether a big commercial portal such as Yahoo! or your own EIP:

1. Eyeballs—Or more accurately the *number* of eyeballs (or number of people) that visit the portal. Whether the site is driven by advertising dollars or not, a portal is always fundamentally concerned with attracting viewers, if only from a very targeted segment or subsegment of the

marketplace (or even your employees). The more eyeballs you get, the more products you'll sell or the better
informed your employees will be (depending upon whose
eyeballs they are).

2. User experience—The way a portal, or any web site for
   that matter, attracts new visitors is by creating a compelling user experience for those using the portal. In other
   words, the more useful or interesting or easy or fun the
   experience is, the more likely it is that people will want
   to go to and return to the portal. How to create a compelling user experience is a combination of Hollywood-
   esque production finesse combined with useful and enter-
   taining content. Essentially, it's all about creating a hyper
   version of CNN, where everything I want to know is
   available to me when I want it and in the form I want it.
   Even though there are a number of consumer portals
   competing for the same eyeballs, and offering similar
   content (Reuters news, stock quotes, weather, sports,
   search engine capabilities, etc.), the successful portals offer an opportunity for users to create a unique personalized experience—for example, My Yahoo! and
   Netscape's My Netcenter allow users to create a personalized Web experience. Users can, for example, create
   "stock portfolios" used to track their stocks (or wish list
   thereof), the way information is organized on their
   screens, which regions they want weather updates on,
   what keywords determine the news they get updated on,
   and so on. The experience can be completely tailored to
   a user's unique, personalized, profile, and, further, this
   profile can be easily adapted as new interests/concerns
   develop.

3. Stickiness—This is the result of a compelling user experience that keeps eyeballs coming back again and again
   because they like what they see. The key element in stickiness is staying up-to-date, which means being real time.
   Remember that Internet shoppers are not patient. If they
   can't get what they want, or they get bored, they'll move
   on. And it's very easy to move on when you're shopping

on the Internet—you don't even have to physically move! To stay sticky, the portal must continue to evolve its value. That, in fact, is another reason portals are essential to the fast-paced world of Internet commerce: They allow constant, rapid evolution and updating, with relatively little cost.

Creating an E-Community

Given that a portal is literally a window to information, a portal has the power to shape its users' views of the world. A well-designed portal can be a very valuable tool in shaping the views of the community you're trying to reach. This represents enormous commercial potential, but it also represents significant social potential. The large commercial portals have been successful because they offer a compelling user experience that is sticky enough to attract and retain eyeballs. If you look at their success in a little more detail, you will see five things they've all done well:

1. Unique—They provide a unique experience and a unique image or brand.

2. Entertain—They have a strong entertainment value, even if they also provide serious information.

3. Create community—They provide a means for people to connect with each other more easily—an evolved form of chat room.

4. Embody our curiosity about ourselves and our world— They feed our sense of wonder and curiosity by giving us expanded access to information about our world.

5. Provide instant gratification—They make getting what we want easier and faster.

There is a more profound phenomenon happening with the advent of these characteristics, because they appeal to very fundamental human characteristics that transcend technology.

Another way to view these characteristics is as fundamental human needs. We all want to:

- Either feel unique or feel uniquely treated

- Be entertained and enjoy perspectives beyond our everyday life

- Be involved with other people and feel part of a community

- Know more about ourselves, each other, and the world we live in (who would really argue that curiosity isn't a fundamental human trait?)

- Have our needs—and even our whims—satisfied immediately

The Internet has, of course, created the potential for many of these needs to be met on a macro level, but the concept of the portal provides the mechanism to achieve these needs on a specific level. The big gains in the acceptance and usability of the Internet really only occurred once the Web, and Web browsers, became prevalent and offered highly graphical presentations of the available content. Web sites and their highly visual, easily understood interfaces took the Internet a step closer to general usability. Similarly, portals make the Internet more active and interactive, allowing users to personalize their experience without jumping from site to site. But as the Internet has unlocked information, it has also accelerated our demands. The closer we get to instant gratification, the more we want it, because "more" seems that much more attainable.

The real value of the portal will come in its ability to extend the concept of electronic, transient communities. Portal communities are environments that can meet the five human characteristics I've outlined. An electronic community is desirable, because it meets our needs for connecting to others while also allowing us to shift from community to community as our personal needs change, without complicated logistics. Indulging our personal interests in this way is also optimal for making us feel unique and giving us an almost perfect sense of personalization.

I've had many programmers over the years explain to me the mindset and culture behind software developers, especially hard core "hackers." For many programmers, the attraction to creating software centered around two key characteristics: the ability to be creative and the ability to be in complete control. There was a real "rush" in being able to create something from nothing—that is, a functioning computer program—and being in complete control of that creation and its environment. In a sense, as a software developer, you are a little god of your world. To many of us, the world of the software developer has often been seen as a subculture with unique characteristics. But I don't see the mindset of the software developer as very different from what we all ultimately exhibit. In this sense, a portal allows any Internet user to feel the creativity and personalization of software technology. Through the portal you can, in both a business and a personal context, create a completely personalized view of the world of the Internet. A good portal allows users to sense the power and control relished by my developer friends via "personalized" services.

The EIP—Your Showroom for the Twenty-First Century

If (or when) you build the EIP for your business, there are six critical elements to consider, as shown in Figure 5.1. As a general rule, the EIP should be based on the same real-time infrastructure technology used by the event-driven enterprise. This technology allows for the scalable, flexible integration infrastructure necessary to connect core business systems with new kinds of services and to serve it all up over the Internet through multiple types of end-user devices. What you end up with is an EIP that serves as the visualization mechanism for all the integrated content within an enterprise, combined with relevant xternal content, to create a rich and beneficial resource and experience for employees, customers, and/or business partners. The six critical components of the EIP are as follows:

1. Internal content—Orders, product information, customer information, sales figures, and related types of information represent content specific to your business and various activities within your business. How much of this gets exposed in the EIP will depend on who the audience is, but if it's an EIP used by your employees, there may a lot of operational content and related services available through the EIP. What matters most about this content is that in an EIP it is the core of what you're trying to deliver—everything else is background. The biggest challenge is getting the content to the EIP in the first place. That's where the event-driven IT infrastructure discussed in Chapter 4 comes into play. That infrastructure allows the content and services of your business systems to be made available to the EIP and extended over the Internet to the users of your EIP. Without this IT infrastructure you can't get at your content or meet the other key performance needs of the EIP.

2. External content—News, stocks prices, weather, sports scores, and so on all represent external types of informa-

Figure 5.1

Enterprise
Information
Portal
components.

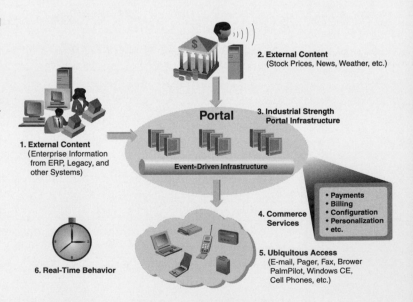

2. **External Content**
   (Stock Prices, News, Weather, etc.)

Portal

3. **Industrial Strength Portal Infrastructure**

1. **External Content**
   (Enterprise Information
   from ERP, Legacy, and
   other Systems)

Event-Driven Infrastructure

4. **Commerce Services**

♦ Payments
♦ Billing
♦ Configuration
♦ Personalization
♦ etc.

5. **Ubiquitous Access**
   (E-mail, Pager, Fax, Brower
   PalmPilot, Windows CE,
   Cell Phones, etc.)

6. **Real-Time Behavior**

tion that most of us are interested in. Some of this information also plays a very real, ongoing part in our decision-making processes, both in our personal lives and in our professional lives. Sports scores may not be that critical to some, but news, weather, and stock prices are often very germane to making a business decision or deciding to take a vacation. I may not choose to sign up a distributor for my products if the news tells me something negative about that company or if its stock price falls precipitously. I also may not decide to take a vacation if a hurricane is predicted for my destination or the value of my stock portfolio is cut in half by a market "correction." All of this external content has become the background for daily decisions, so we want it there all the time, constantly updating. We may not always actively use it, but we don't want to be without it either. It has become our adult security blanket—just look at how many of us receive news and stock quotes on our pagers.

3. Industrial-strength portal infrastructure—Industrial strength means that the EIP can sustain high rates of use and high rates of throughput for the content it provides. Yahoo! Finance, for example, has, because of its industrial-strength infrastructure, handled tens of millions of requests for stock price information, particularly during turbulent days on the stock market. Other, less-robust financial information EIPs and Web sites have failed due to their user load under similar circumstances, helping to boost Yahoo!'s stickiness over its competitors. Achieving an industrial-strength infrastructure constitutes more than simply buying a big server computer for your Web site. The key is a flexible, extendable infrastructure, which can grow as the community you're serving grows. To create this infrastructure, the same core technologies that drive your event-driven enterprise should drive your EIP. This infrastructure also provides all the security and access control capabilities the EIP requires. By using event-driven technology, your EIP infrastructure leverages the benefits of distributed computing to allow multiple com-

puters to work in conjunction with each other. As your
needs grow, more computers can be added.

4. Commerce services—This may seem obvious, but your
   EIP must be able to support key commerce services, such
   as notifications, transactions, payments, profiling, personalization, and cataloging. These are the types of capabilities that enable the EIP to do more than just be a
   directory or search engine, allowing it to be a revenue-
   generating enterprise rather than an IT cost center. EIP
   users can invoke these services to actually buy things, instead of just reading about them. Some of these services
   may actually come from your core business systems.
   Others may be needed to support the specific operations
   of the portal, such as special billing systems or personalization servers. Because the existing and new portal-
   specific services are connected through a common infrastructure, they can be used in an integrated fashion.

5. Ubiquitous access—Over the next decade, the growth in
   wireless communications for many different types of devices will make access through alternative information
   devices more significant than access through the desktop
   PC. We may use our PCs a great deal today, but over the
   next decade our PCs will represent only a small percent-
   age of our total means for accessing the Internet. Moreover, the majority of these devices—even your PC—will
   communicate over wireless networks. The new low-earth
   orbit satellite technology currently being deployed will
   give us unprecedented ubiquitous mobile communications, not just for voice, but also for data and Internet
   access. If your EIP can't leverage these new wireless networks and devices, it will miss what may soon be the
   largest audience available.

6. Real-time behavior—Underlying all of the above-men-
   tioned components of the EIP infrastructure is also the assumption of real-time behavior, without which an EIP
   can become a bit dull. Assuming that Internet users are
   increasingly oriented to getting what they want instantly,
   anything but real time is history. As with industrial

strength, real time is a necessary, but not in itself a sufficient, characteristic of an effective EIP. If it's not there, the EIP user will be disappointed, but once used it is taken for granted. Content consumers are becoming just like financial traders in that they have developed very high service expectations, which, once met, will only generate new requirements. But today, real-time content delivery is as good as it gets (you can't be more up-to-date than real time), so that's what you need to deliver to your customers.

These six characteristics I have described for the EIP involve all the same technology discussed in Chapter 4, as well as the same basic capabilities that drive content distribution inside the event-driven enterprise. The EIP, though, puts a new spin on the basic technology capabilities by using them to allow personalized access through multiple channels. EIPs may not, in themselves, represent fundamentally new technology, but they do represent a new *convergence* of technologies that makes it easier to bring the Internet into your business and to move your business out over the Internet.

An analogy for what I'm advocating on the Internet via portals is the equivalent of a storefront or a showroom that has been arranged to provide customers with a unique and pleasurable experience. A good portal experience is similar to a good bookstore experience. A good bookstore has books, but also newspapers, a message board where related events and reviews can be posted, art on the walls, pleasant music being played or even performed, readings, a coffee bar, comfortable lounge chairs, an information kiosk, CDs, helpful salespeople, and so on. A good bookstore doesn't rely solely on the attractiveness of the books themselves—those are a commodity—a good bookstore focuses on the user experience. The bookstore owners know that the experience is their value-add and their best hope for retaining customers in this world of on- and offline discount bookstores. Similarly, the much talked about online bookstore, Amazon.com, attempts to replicate the bookstore experience over the Web. At Amazon, books may be offered at competitive prices, but the attraction for many is the growing set of related services and content. A sort of literary portal, Amazon gives customers—in addition to books—book reviews and ratings, synopses, chat groups, personalized reading recommendations (based on your indicated interests and buying habits), and more. This is the Internet equivalent of creating a enjoyable physical experience for the book buyer.

Think of your own company's portal as allowing you the opportunity to create a bookstore-type experience for your customers. For those of you who have sold through indirect channels, focusing on the end customers and their buying experiences may be new, but all that has to change in the era of the Internet. You need to learn about who your customers are and cater to them in order to retain them. As an example: Your business is selling online airline tickets. Although you don't make money from booking hotel rooms, selling travel books, recommending museums or restaurants, giving information on current weather conditions, and other travel tips, providing access to this type of content will allow you to sell more tickets, because you have created an entire experience for your customers. You've provided one-stop shopping for their entire vacation, selling, in effect, not just the airline ticket, but the desired weather conditions, scuba gear, beachfront villa, and Caribbean cuisine your customers "uniquely" desire. The portal concept will allow you to apply these same value-added principles to your customers' experience of your e-business, no matter what it is you do—whether it's selling widgets or beanie babies.

I started this chapter explaining the myth of e-business, but I want to finish it by stressing how portals and EIPs can help you capitalize on the enormous potential of the Internet. Don't let the hype surrounding vague concepts of e-business distract you from how an EIP can help you integrate your business with the Internet. With a portal, capitalizing on the Internet is really a natural extension of the infrastructure you've already built to support your event-driven enterprise.

THE EVENT-DRIVEN PHILOSOPHY

To understand the event-driven company's posture toward others, it's important to explore the event-driven company's understanding of itself and the business environment it inhabits. The implementation by an organization of the event-driven architecture usually follows the organization's realization that, to paraphrase Albert Einstein, everything has changed but our way of thinking. Indeed, the world of business has changed so rapidly in so short a time that most executives are still holding true to yesterday's contemporary course when something much more powerful and flexible is required. The event-driven architecture is the first information system that directly ties the flow of information about business events to business logic itself.

Evolution of the business environment gives rise to a new vocabulary, which not only reflects that evolution but signifies new ways of connecting with other players in the environment. For example, throughout this book I speak of "cellular" organizations doing business in an "ecosphere," deploying "inputs" and "outputs" to other cellular entities. These are not just new labels for old concepts or sensitive Silicon Valley–speak—I haven't heard anyone in the Valley use these terms, in fact—but a whole new way of looking at the relationships among business organizations in a time of enormous transformation.

"Contemporary" to "Cellular"

In an attempt to save you time, I haven't bothered in these pages to critique any business form earlier than the "contemporary" structure of the 1990s. This may have irritated some readers, inasmuch as the contemporary company is supposedly the latest and greatest form business can take. In a 1997 article in *Academy of Management Executive,* business logician Raymond E. Miles [48] identifies the key characteristic of the *contemporary* business form as "the extension of the customization process backward and forward along the entire industry value chain, from raw materials, to parts and component production, to manufacture and assembly, to distribution and final sale . . .

outsourcing noncore operations to upstream and downstream partner firms."

You are probably more than familiar with the characteristics Miles ascribes to the contemporary company: "It became difficult to determine where one organization ended and another began. . . . Important customers were invited to participate in new-product development processes, and suppliers were given access to large firms' scheduling and accounting processes. . . . Empowered teams managed not only their internal work processes, but also external relationships with upstream and downstream partners."

Nothing wrong with that description, one might say. The best-selling business management books certainly endorse those elements. What's the problem? For clues, note Miles's choice of descriptors: "value chains," "upstream," and "downstream." We see and hear these words all the time, but in truth the business world has become more complex, three-dimensional, and anarchic than such flat, two-dimensional metaphors can encompass (Figure 6.1). Companies today compete in a

Figure 6.1

Contemporary company structure.

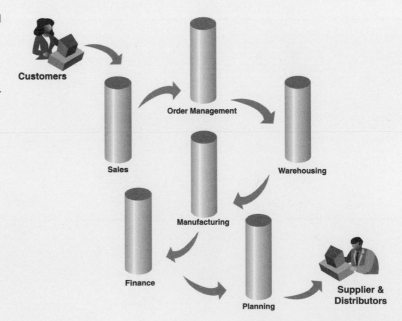

free-form, completely open environment with continuous opportunities to connect not just vertically or horizontally but in all directions at all times: There is no limit, other than the boundaries of entrepreneurial imagination, to the type and number of relationships businesses can maintain. There should be no upstream, no downstream, no value or supply *chains.*

Miles labels the emerging, postcontemporary business structure—of which the event-driven company is an example—a *"cellular organization"* (Figure 6.2), commenting, "The cellular metaphor suggests a living, adaptive organism. . . . A cellular organization is made up of cells (self-managing teams, autonomous business units, etc.) that can operate alone but that can interact with other cells to produce a more potent and competent business mechanism. It is this combination of independence and interdependence that allows the cellular organizational form to generate and share the know-how that produces continuous innovation."

Miles calls the cellular organization's new form of opportunistic, three-dimensional business arrangements "inputs" and "outputs," explaining, "inputs are spread across hundreds and even thousands of [employees] worldwide. . . . Outputs are similarly complex, as myriad [short-term] alliances and partnerships are formed. . . . [This process] . . . creates more and more complex markets and environments."

Figure 6.2
Cellular/open structure.

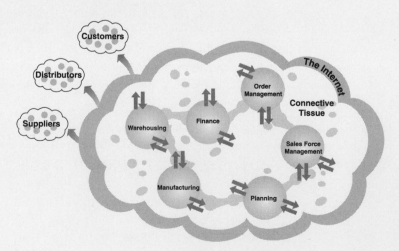

The more profuse and innovative these inputs and outputs become, the more an organization needs to rely on real-time, integrated information as the connecting, collaborative medium of choice. Just as the human body requires complex nervous and circulatory systems to interconnect its cellular structure, the cellular organization requires a complex infrastructure for moving its lifeblood, information, among the various cells of the organization (which can be dispersed around the world). A small, geographically centralized organization can be "cellular" and still function reasonably well without this high-level information system. But once the organization grows beyond 1,000 members (the sum of all "inputs" and "outputs") and experiences geographic dispersion, simple information systems cannot scale up to handle the challenge. At this point, organized means of distributing and exchanging information must be applied.

Until very recently, when the rush to the global networked economy became a stampede, the pace of business did not require much more in the way of information-distribution systems than typical business IT structures and such simple application tools as e-mail or data replication technologies such as LotusNotes. Realizing the full competitive power of the cellular organization in the emerging global networked economy, however, requires technology that integrates the organization's inputs and outputs on a much more fundamental level.

The currently dominant implementation of client/server technology does not provide this infrastructure. The concept of "servers" and "clients" must evolve to a truly distributed information technology architecture—providing active, integrated, real-time information generated by events occurring inside and outside the company—if the cellular organization is to make full use of its own flexible novelty.

"Industry" to "Ecosystem"

The change in view from contemporary to cellular carries with it a concomitant shift in understanding of the business landscape itself. James F. Moore [49] argues that we ought to discard the very word "industry" in favor of something more all-encompassing:

> What we are seeing, in fact, is the end of industry . . . as a useful concept in contemplating business. The presumption that there are distinct, immutable businesses within which players scramble for supremacy is a tired idea whose time is past. It has little to do with what is shaping the world. . . .
>
> In place of "industry," I suggest an alternative, more appropriate term: *business ecosystem*. . . . Business ecosystems span a variety of industries. The companies within them coevolve capabilities around innovation, and work cooperatively and competitively to . . . support the next round of innovation. . . .

The event-driven architecture enables the emerging cellular organization to become potent within its ecosystem by sharing the know-how that produces Moore's continuous innovation and by providing the real-time, relational collaboration without which Miles's cellular organization cannot function. It has the ability to turn his "unpredictability [of multiple] inputs and outputs" into opportunity and the structure (ubiquitous, active information) that provides focus when all else is fluid and chaotic. All of this may sound like the language floating around the lunch room at an Internet start-up company where executives play Frisbee or skateboard at lunch. Not really. This is simply how good business sense sounds at the century's turn.

Navigating Amid Change with No Pattern

The rise of the Internet as a critical business platform completes a process of transfiguring change that began with globalization, free trade, deregulation, and the communications revolution. We're competing today in a real-time, three-dimensional, worldwide, Wild West, open-architecture free-for-all. Changes have no pattern in this strange new world, as London Business School's Charles Handy [50] observes in *The Age of Unreason.* We have entered a period of "discontinuous change," and people will only frustrate themselves looking for logic in all the old places.

Because it is open-architecture, short on rules, and barrier-free, the global business ecosystem is chaotic and complex, part of what Hertford Business School's Ralph Stacey [51] calls a social ecology, a mass entity that is "adaptive [constantly readjusting] rather than deterministic." Therefore, Stacey argues, "A company today must operate on the edge of chaos to be capable of creativity and novelty." M. Mitchell Waldrop [52] defines "the edge of chaos" as "the constantly shifting battle zone . . . where the components of a system never quite lock into place and yet never quite dissolve into turbulence, either. . . . [The edge of chaos] is the one place where a complex system can be spontaneous, adaptive, and alive."

This environment is the clinching argument, in my view, for the strategic necessity of real-time, integrated, active information. While it may not be possible for you to discern patterns in the flux or to plan tactically farther down the road than one's eyes can see, your competitors are operating under the same conditions. In this situation, intelligence (in the military sense of value-added scouting) becomes the paramount differentiator. The purpose of the event-driven infrastructure is to gather intelligence everywhere in your ecosphere it is available; integrate and analyze its content, in real time, into a meaningful portal presentation; and then deliver the freshest "news" in your business sphere to the immediate attention of the people who want and need to know. In a chaotic environment, information becomes a company's lifeline as it walks the edge.

Knowledge Management in the Event-Driven Company

Information is knowledge ore. A fortuitous by-product of the event-driven architecture is a variety of knowledge management systems that, in my view, outperform many of the dedicated knowledge management solutions on the market today. Wary executives shrink from the term "knowledge management," and with good reason. It's a crucial business concept, which was, almost at birth, opportunistically coopted and trivialized by consultants and vendors eager to repackage old wine in new bottles—yesterday's decision-support or help-desk software has become today's knowledge management solution.

Real knowledge management is a key challenge and opportunity. The rapid downsizings of the last 15 years, the dramatic reduction of middle management, and the increasingly nomadic nature of the workforce have combined to strip companies of hard-earned wisdom and experience, what Thomas Stewart [53] calls "intellectual capital." Many companies have sentenced their workers to endless reinventions of the wheel as they relearn a company's ancient wisdom and then leave, consigning the next generation of workers to the same time-wasting, dispiriting task.

True knowledge management lies at the core of the event-driven company. The active information pulsing through the event-driven company is knowledge continuously refined. Everything that a company has ever done is available for publication to those who subscribe, putting the institutional wisdom of the institution on everyone's desktop. Because the event-driven infrastructure elevates the very nature of knowledge from passive to active, becoming event-driven can supercharge a firm's finest previous efforts at knowledge management.

The consulting firm Ernst & Young, for example, has created "Power Packs," tightly organized, highly specialized collections of information organized for its consultants by areas of special interest. There's one for the insurance ecosystem, another for autos, and so on. Ernst & Young's Center for Business Knowledge convenes groups of 6 to 12 partners with special experience in specific areas and then distills their intellectual capital into 50 MB (laptop-friendly) tutorials, which create "instant expertise" when Ernst & Young's field consultants need it. The Power Packs are stored on Ernst & Young's network servers, reports the August 1997 issue of *Fast Company* [54], "where they can be accessed by any employee."

Useful as the Power Packs are in their current state, imagine how much more value they'd deliver if every update were delivered, via publish/subscribe, to interested Ernst & Young consultants. There'd be no need for each employee to remember the existence of the Power Packs and query the server—individually, of course—to see if there was anything new. Instead, active information would arrive at the desk of every Ernst & Young consultant who needed the information whenever fresh developments warranted.

Becoming event-driven, moreover, increases a company's knowledge management capabilities by boosting its "absorptive capacity." Writing in *Administrative Science Quarterly*, researchers Cohen and Levinthal [55] say that a high degree of absorptive capacity predisposes a company toward "proactiv[ity], exploiting opportunities present in the environment. . . . [Conversely,] organizations that have a modest absorptive capacity will tend to be reactive, looking for solutions to problems as they arrive." Cohen and Levinthal measure a company's absorptive capacity by examining the extent of its "interface with the external environment and the transfer of knowledge across and within subunits." By that measure, the event-driven company is rich in absorptive capacity. Interfacing extensively with the external environment and vigorously transferring knowledge across and within subunits *defines* the event-driven infrastructure.

Such a company, in fact, honors Arie de Geus's [56] concept of "the learning company" by improving upon it. The top 29 of 202 Dun & Bradstreet companies compared in a recent University of Southern California study were found to be "miles ahead of their competitors in . . . codifying and databasing knowledge," according to a March 1998 report by the Annenberg School of Communications at the University of Southern California published in the *St. Louis Post-Dispatch* [57]. Calling such companies "knowledge organizations," the report concluded: "The top companies took active steps to inform all employees of that knowledge['s existence]."

Imagine what the enormous extra benefit would be if that passive, databased knowledge were activated and delivered to everyone in those leading companies who'd profit from receiving it. Event-driven companies have no need to add knowledge management modules as another organizational layer. They *are* knowledge management modules.

All from Column A, All from Column B, All from Column C

Contemporary business wisdom holds that competitive excellence derives from choosing a focus and then going deep to exploit it. I certainly have nothing against focus and depth, but one of the greatest advantages to becoming event-driven is that, because they are supported by powerful, active information, event-driven organizations have the strength to maintain breadth and focus simultaneously. This is a good thing, because in today's competitive climate both are required.

Michael Treacy and Fred Wiersema [58] base their book, *The Discipline of Market Leaders: Choose Your Customers, Narrow Your Focus, Dominate Your Market*, on the argument that one must find the "discipline" to choose one from among the following "value propositions" while letting the others slide to "minimal threshold performance levels":

- *Operational excellence* companies provide midmarket products at the best price with the least inconvenience and hassle-free service.

- *Product leadership* companies offer products that push performance boundaries. . . . They continue to innovate year after year. . . .

- *Customer intimacy* adherents focus on delivering . . . what specific customers want. They cultivate relationships. They specialize in satisfying unique needs that only they, by virtue of their close relationship with the customer, recognize.

Two of these three value propositions appeal to me. One, two, or all three might appeal to you. In the event-driven universe, they are not mutually exclusive. Adopting one or two does not bar the others. In fact, today's environment demands most if not all of these superlative characteristics if a company is to survive, much less gain a competitive advantage. The event-driven company will not need to pick one of these value propositions and let the others coast to "minimal threshold levels." All three are within its reach.

Here's another example of necessary all-inclusion that's enabled by the event-driven infrastructure: In his book, Steven E. Gross [59] identifies four distinct "work cultures." One, "functional culture," is the old-fashioned, from-the-top-down 1950s company that everyone claims no longer exists and thus merits no examination. The other three, however, although presented by the author as different forms, are simply variations on the event-driven theme: "In the 'process culture,'" writes Gross, "effectiveness is measured through the eyes of the customer. . . . [There is] continuous improvement. Planning, execution, and control are integrated as close to the customer as possible. Communication is constant, and teams are linked to the [ecosystem] through the decision-making process."

That sounds like an event-driven company.

In Gross's "time-based culture," "companies seek to maximize return on assets [by] dominating their markets through technical prowess, then use the accumulated competencies of their people to move on. . . . Work is designed around management . . . that adds value and cross-functional project teams for the duration of the activity. . . . Individuals are encouraged to develop multifunctional expertise and competencies."

That sounds like an event-driven company, too.

Gross's "network culture" is composed of "ad hoc groups and temporary alliances that bring together the necessary skills to complete a specific venture and cease to exist after its goal is achieved. Priorities are shaped around the need to respond immediately to customers and to create and then penetrate opportunistic market niches. . . . Power in this culture comes from being able to perform critical work and bring the right people together to orchestrate successful outcomes."

That *really* sounds like an event-driven company.

Can an event-driven company realistically aspire to competitive advantage in operational excellence, product leadership, *and* customer intimacy? Can an event-driven company honestly hope to encompass *all* the competencies of time-based, functional, and network cultures? Yes. The classic limitations no longer apply. They were composed before the invention of active information. The event-driven organization, the prime example of what Shell Oil's Arie de Geus [60] calls a "learning company," differentiates itself from earlier forms by employing active information to achieve excellence broadly *and* in depth as it adapts fluidly to developments rippling through its business ecosystem.

Let me repeat: This all-skills virtuosity is no parlor trick, no tearing a phone book in half to impress your friends. It's the minimum any company can accomplish to stay ahead of commoditization. Only companies that have mastered excellence across the business spectrum have a chance to create and hold a competitive advantage. Strength and flexibility are the bedrock philosophies of the event-driven company.

Embedding Your Core Competencies

Long-range strategic planning is based on forecasting the future. In today's global business ecosystem, one may be tempted, therefore, to say "so much for long-range strategic planning." Ralph Stacey [61], the British scholar of complexity, sounds a pessimistic note: "it is impossible to . . . plan a series of actions that will lead to a specified long-term outcome."

All that appears to remain is the limited comfort of maxims: "Win in the short term . . . [ensure] you're in an even stronger position to win in the future" (John Kotter [62]). "Hope for the best. Expect the worst" (Mel Brooks [63]).

Difficult as it may be to forecast the future, the event-driven company can profitably anticipate evolution in its ecosystem via the web that connects the company to other organisms in the ecosystem. Just as, on the micro level, the event-driven infrastructure prompts a Bechtel engineer in San Francisco to change his wiring scheme the moment an architect in Bombay moves an oil refinery's planned wall on the blueprint, on the macro level a top executive at a semiconductor company can consider a change in strategy when presented with real-time analysis of Asian personal computer sales trends and market reports of increasing enterprise orders.

Above all, the active information infrastructure allows event-driven companies to develop an ongoing, one-on-one dialog with their customers and with the forces affecting their customers.

In a complex chaotic environment, long term planning is impossible. All companies can do to promote success, argues Stacey [64], is to remove "obstacles to effective . . . learning in the present . . . [and to focus on] detecting anomalies . . . [and] using intuition . . . to develop responses" to the changing environment. "Success has to be the discovery of patterns that emerge through actions we take in response to the changing . . . issues we identify."

By its nature, the event-driven company is in a position to do exactly that. The benefits of the "monitoring" and "adjusting" Lissack prescribes accrue to both the company and its customers. Event-driven companies know a good deal about their customers' businesses and should develop the expertise to "read" active information creatively to help customers look to their futures. The partnership that results allows the event-driven company to embed its core competencies in customers' processes and logic. Not by locking the core competencies in with a trick or a trap. Rather, the event-driven company embeds its core competencies by making the value of a relationship so increasingly beneficial that customers can't wait to get more entwined. Essentially, embedding core competencies means establishing an electronic umbilical cord with your customers, which both "nourishes" the customer relationship and provides vital feedback to your company about the health of the relationship. Ideally, you remain in continuous touch with your customers, allowing your company to respond instantly to issues and opportunities as they occur.

How 3Com Embeds Its Competencies

3Com Corporation is an example of a company that has embraced the concept of increased customer value through embedded core competencies and the electronic umbilical cord. As with all event-driven companies, 3Com believes that information technology's ultimate purpose is to provide organizations with the ability to acquire, distribute, and exploit information to gain and maintain competitive advantage. 3Com is utilizing real-time integration capabilities to become a leading example of the event-driven company at work.

The benefits to 3Com's customers and employees are manifold—improved customer service; breakthrough improvements in the speed and accuracy of business execution based on real-time, networked information; and increased productivity via instant, customizable access to the personalized information needed to get the job done.

In a marketplace where quality customer service is no longer a differentiator, a company must provide leading-edge service to retain its customers. A large customer of 3Com's needed faster access to vital bug fixes and technical white papers. The customer's requirements drove 3Com to look at how it delivered support information and notified customers on the status of service issues. The result was a state-of-the-art Web service delivery system, which ensured that 3Com's customers would have immediate access to the information they needed.

The 3Com Web service delivery system ensures customers direct access to personalized information. Users define the information they want delivered to them on a regular basis, and the information is automatically posted to their desktops as it becomes available. Customers can select information such as bug reports, release notes, support tips, and user guides on a variety of products. Customers can also monitor their technical support cases online. Customers can make inquiries around the clock and add additional information immediately when a related event occurs and details are fresh. It eliminates the need to make repeated follow-up phone calls and increases the efficiency of both the customer and 3Com technical support engineers.

3Com's business productivity and customer satisfaction have improved dramatically as a result of its commitment to providing customers with the information they need, when they need it.

LEADERSHIP AND ORGANIZATION

Even if you decide to build the exact infrastructure I have described, this will not automatically make your company event-driven any more than buying a treadmill will automatically make you fit. Investing in *things* is just a beginning. The event-driven company, as I suggested at the beginning of this book, is one that develops both the *technical infrastructure* to deliver real-time, active information and the *human infrastructure* to transform that information first into knowledge and then into intelligent, ongoing action. In this chapter, I will detail how the event-driven technical infrastructure enables important shifts in a company's leadership and organizational models—shifts that improve the company's interface to customers and enable increased revenue.

The Star System

The star system, which defines an event-driven company, became possible the moment the information and communications revolution hit workers' desktops. On that day, information left the executive suite and became democratic. It allowed workers to move, as Michael Hammer [65] put it, "from performing a task to achieving results." It put power closer to the customer interface.

A "star" in an event-driven company is a worker, regardless of official rank, who creates superior customer value by combining personal skill sets with the advantages of event-driven information to anticipate a customer's need (often before the customer realizes the need) and then fills this need with the most inventive, highest-quality product or service at the highest possible margin. "Margin" does not only refer to the company's profit. The worker, too, must feel well rewarded. Employees must always be afforded the opportunity to grasp a sense of shared ownership and reward. All management can do is *intend* worker empowerment and help each worker on the path toward grasping empowerment. After that, it's up to the worker. Stars will grasp successfully.

Because I selfishly want to keep my stars, I encourage my employees to always look out for their own bottom lines as well as the company's. They are constantly assessing: What can I learn from this experience? How can I improve my own networking? What skills have I upgraded? If workers feel as though they're getting a good deal, they'll put out their best efforts. As I said earlier, the best value any worker can get from his or her employer these days is not lifetime *employment* but lifetime *employability*.

Crucial in the star's personal skill set is an old-fashioned devotion to *personal* customer service and satisfaction. Now that near-twenty-first-century machines are capable of addressing multiple markets, workers are obliged to return to classic, nineteenth-century, one-on-one service concepts. Though banks and other large institutions are currently spending hundreds of millions on automation software that will allow them to chat knowingly and personably with their best customers, one rude phone rep will instantly reduce the ROI of these systems to zero. Stars, it goes almost without saying, are never rude.

They are never rude to customers, that is. Within their company's walls, however, stars sometimes *are* rude and ruthless in crusading for their customers. And, to be frank, there's a little of the prima donna, the franchise-player athlete, the brilliant if abrasive jazz soloist, in a star. Enjoying, even encouraging the sometimes difficult attitude of top value-creators is a signature characteristic of the event-driven company. Contemporary companies shy away from brilliant-but-difficult types. They pride themselves on assembling team players, who, I suppose, produce a pleasant Muzak hum. But I believe an entire organization is galvanized to excellence by the presence in its midst of great jazz soloists, who are constantly inventing ways to satisfy their customers. Yes, great soloists may have some foibles, and they may sometimes be hard to take. But I've yet to see a statue erected to honor an anonymous member of the horn section. As we will see, it is the leadership's job to keep all of the "soloists" moving forward toward a common intent.

Your company's stars are workers who use the advantages of the event-driven information system to become the equivalents of profit-seeking traders—hyper-aware, entrepreneurial, victory-obsessed, tireless, and ingenious. In the event-driven company, there's no reason everyone should not become a star (at least from time to time, if not continuously). As Peter Drucker [66] said, in the Information Age "there are no excuses for nonperformance" for the simple reason that knowledge is "universally accessible."

Thomas Stewart [67], in *Intellectual Capital,* defines stars as:

> [People] whose talent and experience create the products and services that are the reason customers come to one company and not to a competitor. The greater a company's percentage of high value-added work performed by hard-to-replace people, the more it can charge for its services and the less vulnerable it is to competitors, because it will be even more difficult for rivals to match these skills than it is for the first company to replace them.

Stars in companies will wax and wane depending on the challenges. A customer champion might arise on a given project—from sales, from engineering, from the shipping department—and galvanize everyone by having the bright ideas, seeing the paths to solutions, and exhibiting the passion to inspire others to join the fight. Wise managers will use their power over resources to give the star and his or her followers whatever's needed to keep the fires burning, and then get out of the way. When the project is over, the star may return to excellent but not incandescent performance as another star ignites. This phenomenon has been observed by the complexity theorists at the Santa Fe Institute; they call it "flocking."

Flocking is an organization's ability to recognize and take advantage of opportunities by flexibly mobilizing resources *immediately* around those opportunities, much as birds will rotate leadership of their flying wing when one bird tires and another one takes over as the next, best hope. Creative failure plays an important role in successful flocking. A star may emerge, lead a charge in what turns out to be the wrong direction, and then fall back as event-driven feedback shows that another approach is necessary. There's nothing negative about failure if everyone can learn from it and then flock around a new idea and a new star. Challenging stars to try things that fail, and then supporting them when failure strikes, is one of the most difficult but rewarding skills managers can develop. Fortunately, the event-driven company is bathed in a constant flow of real-time results feedback, allowing failure to be detected and corrected swiftly enough to consider it a form of learning. These failures can be determined by applying a system of matrixes, or rules, that looks for key performance indicators, such as sales numbers, inventory levels, or cost margins. The essence of event-driven failure-management is to strike quickly in reversing experimental ideas that aren't working.

A uniquely event-driven star skill is the ability to surf information waves. Although the event-driven infrastructure contains filtering mechanisms to protect workers from drowning in data, as well as permission and security mechanisms that control the flow of certain types of information, most people will still need to use their human abilities to decide which exceptional exception requires immediate attention because it is the most exceptional of all.

The true star will be the worker who effectively interprets the information available to him or her and who surfs external data sources for critical and relevant news and information. At TIBCO, for example, we have a number of internal and external information channels that employees can subscribe to. There is a sales channel, a solutions channel, a product channel, a support channel, and so on. Each channel is designed to provide employees in certain realms, or business units, with the information that they most need to succeed at their jobs. Additionally, there are a series of external channels, such as Industry Update, which scrapes content from competitor Web sites and integrates news stories from Reuters data feeds, as well as a public channel that scrapes headlines from Reuters news, *USA Today*, and weather sources. Stars at TIBCO and elsewhere will shape their information flows to maximize the chance of learning something relevant and important.

If the worker isn't getting the right information, the fault does not lie with the event-driven infrastructure but with the way it is being deployed: With myriad information sources from inside and outside the enterprise linked and integrated, the event-driven environment is potentially the most news- and

content-intensive in the world. The key is to subscribe to the
right information. This requires that the worker take the initiative to change his or her filters on the information flow; continuously evaluating and reevaluating the choices available for that
information will provide new insight. An event-driven environment doesn't miraculously tell you what you need to know,
but it makes it possible for the motivated knowledge worker to
find it.

Compensation, Partnership, and Ownership

The star system requires an approach to compensations and rewards that's as fluid as the work environment itself. Obviously,
every worker in the company should be creating more than
enough value to cover his or her own compensation. Stars, however, require more than mere compensation. The classic relationship between workers and management has changed in the
age of the ubiquitous knowledge economy, when potential stars
are less plentiful than good jobs. Competitive pay scales are important, but, as with Porter's old competitive differentiators,
what was once good enough to win is now simply the basic
price of entry to the competition. A handsome paycheck may
get people through your door, but it takes far more to hold the
stars who can separate your company from the competition.

I applaud workers today for wanting to be decision-making
partners, for wanting to know why something is being asked of
them before they do it, even to challenge authority in a manner
that would be seen as terminal insubordination in a hierarchical
company. It is not an altogether bad thing that we're living in a
"what's in it for me?" world in which company and worker transcend the old myth of mutual loyalty to create a system of mutually beneficial value exchanges that include all manner of
nonmoney perks.

As Thomas Stewart [68] points out, there's a paradox at work
in Information Age companies:

> At the same time that employers have weakened the ties of job security and loyalty, they more than ever depend on human capital. . . . The most valuable knowledge workers are the best able to leave their employers, taking their work with them. Knowledge workers, for their part, because they bring to their work not only their bodies but their minds—even their souls—are far more loyal to their work, though not to their employer.

The phenomenon of people caring deeply about their work is not restricted to Silicon Valley–type firms or to white-collar workers only. In *The Deming Management Method*, Mary Walton's [69] account of Ford's breakthrough Team Taurus development effort, Team Taurus leader Lew Veraldi talks about consulting "hourly workers" on assembly lines about how to make the Taurus easier to build. The process yielded thousands of suggestions, most of which Ford incorporated. Walton quotes Veraldi: "It's amazing the dedication and commitment you can get from people just by seeking their involvement."

Thomas Stewart [70] accurately observes that "ceding ownership of human capital to a corporation must be voluntary" if the star employee is to remain. To make this cession as enthusiastic as possible, he proposes "creating a sense of cross-ownership between employee and company," quoting Charles Handy's suggestion that corporations be seen as "membership communities" to which there is a "sense of belonging" in order "to hold people to the corporation."

Warm and fuzzy rhetoric can only go so far in this effort before we're back at the old loyalty myth. Giving people exciting work to do, encouraging them while they're doing it, intending them to grasp a sense of partnership and equality, allowing for extensive goal and ownership opportunities, and recognizing people's efforts and offering them a continuous banquet of skill upgrades are all good beginnings. Monetary rewards play an important role, as well, but not primarily in the form of large salaries.

Salary is short-term compensation, and those who focus on it are usually short-term thinkers, not long-term value creators. Although the event-driven company lives in real time and considers speed one of its prime competitive advantages, its star employees usually turn out to be people who take a long-term view of value creation. As I mentioned earlier, the event-driven company is organized around long-term *intent* with an eye more on tomorrow's revenues than today's.

The stars I want on my team, therefore, have no problem remaining with a company that pays them salaries around the 60th percentile of comparable firms if much larger rewards are made available—in well-publicized ways—for sustained value creation in the long term.

Annual bonuses are excellent ways to match long-term value creation with financial reward. Bonuses should be based on the company's overall performance, the performance of specific projects in which the worker has been involved, and the overall satisfaction of customers—as expressed by the customers themselves.

Surveying customers directly about their satisfaction delivers multiple dividends. You get priceless feedback on how you look to others—something even event-driven information can rarely tell you—and customers appreciate being asked their views of your people who are serving them. The process often turns customers into evangelists for your employees! When it comes to surveying your customers, never proceed on the assumption that no news is good news. Always ask.

I consider each of my employees the CEO of the minicompany within the larger company—the subcell within the larger cellular structure—that serves a certain set of customers via a certain set of projects for a certain period of time. If that minicompany does well, then the CEO deserves a CEO-sized bonus. To keep the stars I need, I've found that it is imperative that the "potential" bonus places the employee's total compensation in the 98th percentile. Stars will accept average salaries against the hope of superlative bonuses, if they know excellent work will reward them with a compensation package (salary and bonus) that is competitive.

Equity, the longest-term compensation of all, raises new sets of questions. It has become commonplace in Silicon Valley for cash-strapped start-up firms to "pay" stars with large blocks of stock, which, in time, either prove worthless or make their owners shockingly wealthy. The incentive is tremendous. Start-up firms are filled with would-be millionaires who move into their offices and work 16-hour days. This may be incentive toward the wrong goal: burnout. Nevertheless, sharing bedrock equity with the stars who create value must be part of an event-driven company's compensation structure, even for long-established firms that can't simply grant millions of options. Stars will stay longest, and create the most value, if they have a literal chance to experience the "cross-ownership" Stewart proposes.

The best policy is to blend incentive and reward equity: incentive to jump-start a star's commitment to the event-driven company's entrepreneurial culture and reward to recognize the actual creation of value and "pattern" employees to keep on creating value over the long term.

No matter what blend of incentives and rewards you choose, it's essential that employees have the opportunity to empower themselves to meet expectations and earn their extras. It is counterproductive to dangle a big, sweet carrot without giving the workers paths to reach it. It is effective for leaders to customize a bonus plan, setting specific goals for each subcell of the organization to stretch toward sales increases, for example, or quantitative improvements in customer satisfaction and/or retention.

Having discussed workers, we now come to leaders, which, for the event-driven company, is the appropriate order. The proper role of business leaders at the turn of the twenty-first century was outlined in the sixth century B.C., by Lao-tze: "to lead, follow." The leader has assembled a team of stars and an information system that will direct at the team a steady flow of active information. How, in this context, can the event-driven manager best lead by following?

In old and new hierarchical companies, the leader's role is clear-cut: the boss. But in the event-driven company, defining leadership becomes trickier even as the role of the leader becomes more pivotal. The event-driven company has been freed from prior constraints, which is good. Those constraints, inflexible as they were, at least offered structural expectations that defined leadership without the leaders themselves having to do much more than color inside the lines. The nature of leadership in an event-driven company, on the other hand, changes dramatically. The event-driven company is competing in a complex, chaotic ecosystem to which it must adapt advantageously. Which levers should the leaders touch, and which should they leave alone?

The event-driven infrastructure's constant flow of information plays a unique role in finding and honing firmly to the profitable border of chaos that lies between outdated ways of doing business, on one hand, and uncontrolled anarchy, on the other. This holds true for the issue of leadership, as well. The unifying gravitational force of active information shared universally within an organization provides the answer to a question posed by G. Hamel and C. K. Prahalad [71]—to wit, "are there limits to [worker] empowerment?" They write:

> The goal is not simply to reduce organizational levels. . . . The goal is to grant individuals the freedom to . . . satisfy a customer. Yet, are there limits to empowerment? We believe that empowerment without a *shared sense of direction* can lead to anarchy.
>
> While bureaucracy can strangle initiative and progress, so too can a large number of empowered but unaligned individuals who are working at cross-purposes. Every employee should be empowered, but empowered to do what? The notion of a shared direction, what we call *strategic intent*, reconciles the needs of individual freedom and concerted, coordinated effort. . . . Employees want a sense of direction just as much as they want the freedom of empowerment.

It is the role of the event-driven company's leader to provide strategic intent while still allowing the workers to seize their own empowerment. Here the leader, metaphorically, is a gardener: having a strategic intent but acknowledging which forces can be bent to that intent and which, for any number of reasons, are beyond his or her control. The redistribution of power from hierarchy to customer interface in such a system cannot be successful simply because leaders announce that the organization is now flat or inverted and the workers are now empowered. This is where I draw the distinction between leadership in contemporary and event-driven companies. Typical contemporary leaders empower their workers. Event-driven leaders inspire workers to *take* power, to empower themselves. This is the only way true empowerment can occur.

Leadership descriptors abound. In *The Age of Unreason*, Charles Handy [72] describes one CEO who sees himself as a "traffic cop, orchestra conductor, interpreter, critic, and cheer-leader." In *The Drucker Foundation: The Leader of the Future* [73], members of the Peter Drucker Institute define a leader (with deceptive understatement) as someone who has followers, gets results, sets examples, and takes responsibility. C. William Pollard [74] suggests the image of "the leader who serves." Sometimes I think of myself as leader of a jazz band made up of great improvisational players, encouraging each player to take solos while always keeping in mind the melodic theme and the tempo.

The event-driven leader is well imagined as a movie produc-er, the figure who commands the highest-level overview of all projects currently underway, as well as an understanding of all constituent aspects of each individual project. Thanks to the continually refreshed arrival of active information in the event-driven enterprise, the producer/leader has a clear view of the seemingly chaotic environment.

That view is also clearer because it is multidimensional. Drawn from many independent sources, active information solves a leadership problem Tom Peters [75] calls "information distortion" by providing a "requisite variety" of data sources: "The variety of your sources must match the complexity of the real problem, or you will be led to erroneous conclusions." The producer knows best when to seek talent within the organiza-tion or to go virtual, extending an "input/output" to another or-ganism in the ecosystem.

The leader, like the producer, has the institutional clout and the historical perspective to put appropriate central resources—including the leader's own time and support—at project teams' disposal, confirming by his or her actions that power truly re-sides with the teams.

This modeling behavior is important. Reducing bureaucracy and inverting organizational charts are just half the journey to worker empowerment. The other half is putting real power out there for stars to grasp and successfully *intending* them to grasp it. The smartest producers, like the smartest leaders, know how to assemble the best teams and then let it happen—always mon-itoring, never interfering, intervening only by exception.

The Mission Statement: Guiding Star

The leader's "strategic intent" is made manifest in the mission statement, the only part of the event-driven company that is not event-driven. The mission statement is the company's immutable goal, unchanged by any of the setbacks that are inevitable in trying to reach it—or, conversely, by reaching it too soon. NASA's "Land a Man on the Moon" mission statement, once considered far-fetched, was fulfilled in 1969, and NASA has been seeking an equally inspiring mission ever since.

A mission statement should be close to an impossible dream, but not one that *seems* impossible. Christopher Meyer [76] quotes Charles R. Schwab president Dave Pottruck: "Employees are always asking me when is it going to let up? Never. There's no destination that we're going to get to. Thinking that someday we're going to arrive on some pinnacle just isn't going to happen. You've got to enjoy the journey."

For that reason, your company's mission statement ought to be a grand philosophical call to sacrifice and eventual victory that reminds workers that struggle, like the journey, is part of the reward. G. Hamel and C. K. Prahalad [77] tell of the Apple minions who created the personal computer revolution by bringing first the Lisa and then the Macintosh to market: "Many of them look back on those feverish endeavors as the most rewarding years of their professional lives." Your company's mission statement should offer your workers the same chance.

On an operational level, strong mission statements help companies move real power to the customer interface. If everyone in the company has an explicit idea of the company's destination, workers on the value-creation front lines can make decisions and take actions without constantly checking with a boss. A clear vision statement does more in this regard than a much-ballyhooed but largely cosmetic revision in the organizational chart. At TIBCO we have a straightforward vision statement against which our employees can test any contemplated action. If the action seems consistent with the vision, I want my people to take it.

Mission statements can be powerful engines. Yet, companies often fritter away that potential by paying little attention to what their mission statements, properly crafted, can accomplish. G. Hamel and C. K. Prahalad [78] tell this story:

> Recently one of us made a presentation to the top 15 officers of a large multinational company. We showed them their company's mission statement. No one demurred; yes, that looked like their mission statement. *Only, what was on the screen was actually the mission statement of their major competitor!*
>
> What value is a mission statement, we asked, if it is totally undifferentiated? What chance does it offer to stake out a unique and defensible position in an already crowded market?
>
> Why should employees care about a garden-variety mission statement? A strategic intent should offer employees the enticing spectacle of a new destination. . . . Strategic intent must be a goal that commands the respect and allegiance of every employee. . . . Too many mission statements fail entirely to impart any sense of *mission*. . . . Strategic intent is as much about the creation of meaning for employees as it is about the establishment of direction. . . . Every employee has the right to feel that he or she is contributing to the building of a legacy—something of value that is bigger and more lasting than anything that one could accomplish on one's own.

In *Leading Change,* John P. Kotter [79] offers sound ideas for what a mission statement should and should not be. It should not be a narrow financial goal—"15 percent growth in earnings"—that resonates differently within various subcells of the organization and gives employees no clue how their actions will take them or the company there. It should not be a four-inch-thick handbook describing the "Quality Program." It should not be a list of vague, positive values that provide no clear direction: "We stand for integrity, safe products, a clean environment, good employee relations, and so on."

Instead, a company's mission statement ought to engage the hearts and minds of workers because it is derived, pure and true, from the deepest principles and beliefs of the people who created the company. John Kotter's [80] characteristics for effective vision statements include the following:

■ They convey an imaginable picture of what the future—the far future—will be like.

- They appeal to the long-term interests of people with a stake in the firm.

- They consist of realistic, attainable goals.

- They are clear enough to guide decision making.

- They are flexible enough to allow individual initiative.

- They are easy to explain.

TIBCO Software's mission statement is as follows: "To empower every information worker to easily access all the information assets of the corporate environment." In other words, to offer the necessary tools for making any company event-driven. How do Kotter's criteria play through?

- The mission is imaginable, but upon reflection you realize it will take a long, long time to make *all* assets *easily* accessible to *every* information worker.

- The mission appeals to the long-term interests of our workers and organizational partners, because in working toward it everyone can do ground breaking, rewarding work that will change the world's business ecosystem and, as a by-product, make a good deal of money.

- The goal, while aggressive, is attainable, because "all assets," though numerous, are not infinite.

- The mission statement is clear enough to guide decision making: Will the action we are considering empower workers to access corporate information or not?

- Finally, the mission statement *seems* easy to explain because it's deceptively simple: Sure, go ahead, make all the information assets of the corporate environment accessible to every information worker. It's only when you stop to consider what's really being said that the scope of the vision and technical complexity of the challenge emerge.

As I said previously in this chapter, making the transition from any other form to event-driven is similar to changing from fission energy to fusion: Instead of consuming assets, the process creates fresh assets. By putting "all the information assets of the corporate environment" in the hands of information workers—which, these days, is all workers—a company creates a competitive advantage that grows sharper the more it's used.

Tips on How to Lead by Following

Leading by following is far more challenging than leading by bossing. Simply knowing what's going on in the organization is no longer the challenge it once was: The event-driven leader has a bird's-eye view of the ecosystem delivered by intelligently filtered active information. The challenge is finding just the right grip and stance to serve those creating value at the customer edge of the company. Throughout his book, business consultant Douglas K. Smith [81] endorses the following:

- Ask questions instead of giving answers.
- Provide opportunities for others to lead you. Be open to being led.
- Do real work in support of others. Get your hands dirty in aid of the company's mission. Few contribute who only lead or only follow. The greatest contribution comes from those who lead *and* follow.
- Become a matchmaker instead of a "central switch." Don't position yourself as the hub through which all decisions flow. Instead, help others find collaborators to make their own decisions.
- Seek common understanding instead of consensus. Help people understand a project and what it means to the company's mission. Once people understand a project, they may come over to your view or they may not, but the work they do will be fueled by deeper commitment and knowledge.

The leader's role in the event-driven enterprise is as crucial as it ever was in the days of hierarchical corporate structure. The leader, though he or she may be a star employee, must also be a team player, ready to support, listen to, and learn from those he or she manages. The leader's role is to communicate the collective goals and vision necessary to galvanize the forces and motivate the stars.

Leaders in the event-driven corporation must ask themselves a whole new set of leadership questions: Do my employees know what they need to know to succeed? Are they sufficiently informed about the goals of the organization? Are these goals inspirational? Are my employees motivated by their compensation package? How can I help make work more productive for them?

Attaining a role of leadership within the event-driven organization does not signal the beginning of having others serve you. Instead, the success of leaders within the event-driven company is measured by how many of their "reports" become stars, by how often they are outshone by those "below" them.

THE ECOSYSTEM: COMPETITORS, CUSTOMERS, AND PARTNERS

Competitors: A Fine Distraction

Paying too close attention to one's competitors can distract you from paying close enough attention to your customers. One certainly should not ignore competitors, but too many executives become obsessed with matching or beating competitors, at which point ego grabs the wheel from wisdom. Earlier, I cited the examples of perfectly profitable companies with excellent products—Novell and Informix among them—that became obsessed with competitors (Microsoft and Oracle, respectively), lost their customer focus, and eventually lost their trousers. It's better to know what your customers want for breakfast than what your competitors served.

Focusing on your customers can protect your company from being leapfrogged by the competition. If you are intimately connected to your customers via an event-driven information system and putting most of your effort toward solution invention for those customers, you'll know exactly what your customers need even before they do (if you're good at your business). If a competitor manages to leapfrog you in terms of product, you can usually co-opt that one superior product and make it part of your total solution package, or cooperate and compete with that competitor (otherwise known as co-opetition). Your customer will probably be relieved to get the best product (your competitor's) delivered by the designer of the best solution (yours). Solutions that help your customers realize their dreams create more value than brilliant products looking for problems to solve.

Customer focus does not mean being totally subserviant to your customer, or waiting to be told what your customer needs. If you do that, you'll be *treated* like a waiter and dismissed with a $2 tip. To win, you must lead your customers along the path you are building to their dreams. The competitive advantage of the event-driven infrastructure, properly integrated with your customers' IT systems, is that you, and your customer, will have visibility into relevant areas of each others' businesses in real time (e.g., customers might receive information on promotional sales offered by you; you might receive information regarding inventory shortfalls in your customers' systems). Not only will each of you have access to such information, but the relevant information will be directed to the appropriate people within each of your organizations.

This information transparency and constant, event-driven interchange between you and your customer is a high-level iteration of what the marketing scholars Don Rogers and Martha Peppers [82] call a "Learning Relationship," which, in their view, creates "a barrier that makes it more difficult for a customer to be promiscuous than to remain loyal." The event-driven architecture enables the establishment of strong, content-rich Learning Relationships with your customers. Can a company pay too much attention to its customers? I don't think so, but G. Hamel and C. K. Prahalad [83] do. Writing before the advent of the event-driven company, they did not foresee the creative dynamic of the event-driven Learning Relationship. They admonish:

> [A] company must be much more than customer-led. Customers are notoriously lacking in foresight. Ten or 15 years ago, how many of us were asking for cellular telephones, fax machines and copiers at home, 24-hour discount brokerage accounts, multivalve automobile engines, compact disk players, cars with navigation systems, hand-held global satellite positioning receivers, automated teller machines, MTV, or the Home Shopping Network?

Respectfully, my reply to Hamel and Prahalad is: all of us! We were all asking for everything you listed. You are confusing *products* with *solutions*. Every product in the list above is a solution to a customer need. In each case, somebody had a Learning Relationship with customers and was listening. All of us wanted to make telephone calls on the go instead of being tethered to cords attached to walls or to pay phones that are broken as often as not. We wanted the conveniences of office machines available at home. We wanted to play the market whenever we wanted to and pay less for the "privilege" of gambling with our own money. We wanted more powerful, more reliable car engines that used less space and less gas and smaller, better-sounding, nonscratching music storage and playback systems. We wanted to find out where we were without having to pull over or leave the car to ask directions, get money whenever and wherever we wanted to, add a visual component to the audio of pop radio, and shop from home via TV. We knew what we wanted. We just didn't know how to go about getting it.

Hamel and Prahalad are correct to warn us when being "customer-led" refers to the kind of closed-loop market research that forces consumers, acting in a vacuum, to imagine a better future based on their own limited experiences and competencies in the present. This is the kind of customer feedback that leads to banal television situation comedies, radio formats consisting primarily of songs listeners have heard before, and political "platforms" built of the 25 popular poses voters tell pollsters they like most. This kind of feedback loop is the opposite of the event-driven, *keizan teian* loop, because in this loop everything is continually downgraded.

In the event-driven, open feedback loop, everything is continually *upgraded*. The beneficial Learning Relationship dialog with customers feeds into the skills and competencies of the event-driven company and its star value creators. What comes out the other side of this creative process are the innovative products and services Hamel and Prahalad say no customer asked for. But if the event-driven company is in proper touch with its customers, its customers will rarely be obliged to *ask* for anything. Products and services will be in the midst of being invented before those customers are even able to formulate the request.

Intuit Knows How We Feel about Our Money

One event-driven company that engages in just such an anticipatory, constantly upgraded Learning Relationship with its customers is Intuit, which, through its flagship product, Quicken, has been incredibly successful in helping its customers realize their dreams of privacy and convenience in handling their money. Intuit, in fact, exemplifies another key strategy of the event-driven company: embedding its core competencies in customers and partners and allies. Using a Learning Relationship to listen to and lead its customers, Intuit learned exactly how consumers feel most comfortable and in control handling and managing their money over a network. Then Intuit set about embedding that core competence by offering the precise services customers want about two seconds before the customers become conscious of the need.

The earliest versions of Quicken software met a simple, powerful customer demand: to transfer personal finance record keeping from the world of paper into the digital realm. Through keyboard inputting of data gathered from paper, early Quicken customers could maintain computerized checkbooks, track credit-card expenditures, reconcile monthly statements, monitor brokerage accounts, and keep track of their tax records. This was not much by today's standards, but customers appreciated Quicken's customer sensitivity, evidenced by such things as Quicken's intuitive, easy-to-use interface. Intuit's Learning Relationship with its customers alerted the company that Quicken users would embrace features designed for the emerging networked world. Keeping one's records in an isolated computer and typing entries by hand was not enough. As early as 1993, long before the Internet became the popular shopping mall it is today, Intuit began building forward-looking online capabilities into Quicken (Figure 8.1). Among the goals Intuit set for itself were to deliver banking, credit-card, and securities information to customers in as close to real time as possible and to insert this

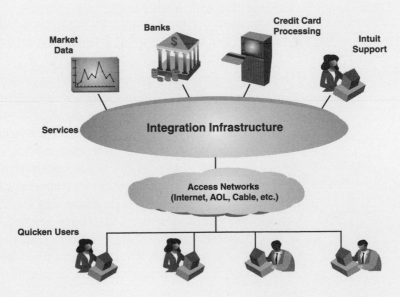

Figure 8.1

Intuit financial services hub.

information into Quicken's registers and analytical features automatically, through the computer. Intuit elected to achieve these goals by creating an information "hub," similar to the hub discussed in Chapter 3, into which financial services providers could publish information and from which Quicken users could extract the data needed to keep their records up-to-the-minute.

To do this, and to achieve scalability—being able to handle crowds of new users—Intuit built an early version of the publish/subscribe infrastructure. Into the hub, financial institutions published encrypted information about Quicken customers' bank, credit-card, and brokerage accounts, as well as real-time securities and financial quotes, all triggered by discrete "events"—a check clears, a credit-card charge is posted, a stock price changes. Intuit assigned each online customer a "proxy" machine, which subscribed to and collected all information requested by the customer while the customer was offline. When the customer logged on and contacted the proxy machine, it fed all the gathered information into the appropriate Quicken tables.

This was, as I said, before the Internet. Intuit used the private (X.25) data networks of telephone companies for the first versions of Quicken online. Beginning in 1995, Quicken customers started migrating to the Internet. In keeping with the event-driven organism's preference for open architectures, in 1997 Intuit and other firms created the Open Financial Exchange (OFX), an international standard that allows the free, platform-independent exchange of data among the world's financial institutions. OFX is attached to the Intuit hub, from which Quicken customers subscribe to whatever event-driven information they need to manage their personal finances in real time.

Intuit's Learning Relationship and the embedding of its core competencies have allowed the relatively small company to hold off serious challenges by Microsoft, which distributes its competing Money software essentially free of charge with the millions of personal computers that come preloaded with Microsoft operating systems. That consumers will pay between $29 and $40 (depending on features) for Quicken when Money comes free is the greatest testament to how deeply Intuit has embedded itself in its customers' lives.

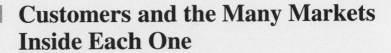

Customers and the Many Markets Inside Each One

As Don Peppers and Martha Rogers [84] point out in *The One-to-One Future: Building Relationships One Customer at a Time,* the very essence of contemporary marketing implies an "adversarial" relationship between a company and its potential customers. Marketers aim at "targets" and conduct "share wars" complete with advertising "blitzes" and gauge the efficiency of their approaches "against" the audience. Potential customers are "exposed" to marketing messages as if they were biological weapons.

As a cellular entity in an interdependent ecosphere, the event-driven company does not engage in contemporary marketing executed with martial strategies. The event-driven company uses the capabilities of its active information infrastructure to go beyond the contemporary concept of markets of one to find and serve multiple markets *within* one customer. Seeking the many markets within each customer returns marketers to their roots: taking goods to the marketplace to meet customers and please them on the spot.

The ancient marketer was event-driven long before the advent of electricity, much less computers. It was possible to be event-driven without mechanical aid when the entire marketplace consisted of several hundred people. The ancient marketer engaged in short-term and long-term Learning Relationships with customers to anticipate the evolution of customer tastes and prepare for patterns of customer demand (e.g., showing Mrs. Jameson the best cuts of meat on Thursdays, because that's when her mother-in-law dines with her family) kept the best customers satisfied by saving the best goods for them, factored in the success of the growing or breeding season to project what crops to plant or what livestock to breed, and haggled to set the highest-margin pricing.

The event-driven infrastructure allows today's marketer to rediscover these capabilities on a global scale, to a cozy local market of billions. Once the event-driven marketer realizes it is possible to create a Learning Relationship dialog with customers and address their current and future needs as intimately and as knowledgeably as the ancient marketer did, many of the precepts of contemporary marketing suddenly seem coarse, blunt, and unfocused.

There's a big financial benefit in finding and serving multiple markets within one customer rather than hoping to attract a steady stream of new customers: Income generated from a steady customer earns far greater margin than income from a new customer. That this is true seems obvious—new customers require greater outlays for marketing, start-up costs, and so on. The *degree* to which it is true is startling. According to Frederick Reichheld's [85] *The Loyalty Effect*, companies *double their profit margins* when business from existing customers increases by as little as 5 percent.

To paraphrase Don Peppers and Martha Rogers [86]:

- In contrast to developing a *product* and trying to find customers for that product, the event-driven marketer develops a *customer relationship* and tries to find product solutions for that customer.

- In contrast to relying on *product managers*, who sell one product at a time to as many customers as possible, the event-driven marketer relies on *customer managers*, who sell as many products and services as possible to one customer at a time.

- In contrast to differentiating products, the event-driven marketer differentiates customers.

- In contrast to trying to acquire a steady stream of new customers, the event-driven marketer tries to generate a steady stream of new business from existing customers.

- In contrast to concentrating on economies of scale, the event-driven marketer concentrates on economies of scope.

The ancient verities of grass-roots marketing were buried by the nineteenth-century enthusiasm for the bigness and standardization of such mass brands as Ford, Coca-Cola, and Sears. Just as the incremental improvement of office technology that resulted in smaller and smaller computers drove corporate power closer to the customer, incremental improvement in marketing technology slowly unearthed and reestablished the truths of the ancient marketer. From the famous "one color suits all" of Henry Ford, marketers discovered segments, then niches, and, finally, "mass customization." But mass customization stopped at the market of one. There is one step left to take.

Writing in the *Harvard Business Review* in 1997, James H. Gilmore and B. Joseph Pine II [87] explained:

> [T]he journey does not end with every customer being his or her own market. The next step, a widespread recognition that multiple markets reside within individual customers, will turn the entire notion of markets and customers completely inside out. . . . Only those companies that take their approach to customization down to this level will gain access to the multiple markets within each of us.

In Chapter 1, I mentioned my long-held conviction that A. G. Bayer, seeking the many markets within this customer, would someday develop "Vivek's Bayer Aspirin," customized for my needs during various segments of the day and week: a dash of clarity added on weekday mornings, a bit of relaxation added at night, a splash of vigor for Saturday night socializing, and so on.

This superfine approach to product and service invention is the future of marketing. You probably prefer to read different sections of the newspaper depending on what day of the week it is, or even which part of the same day you pick it up (business page in the morning, movie listings at night). One day you want to buy a business suit, another day you want to buy hiking gear. J. H. Gilmore and B. J. Pine II [88] report that airlines, hotels, and car rental companies get different requests from the same customers depending on whether they are traveling for business or leisure and what leg of the journey they are on. Business people flying to a sales pitch might order pot after pot of coffee; then, on the homebound leg, champagne (if things went well) or something stronger (if they didn't).

The keys to serving markets of less than one are information, feedback, and collaboration. The customer and the marketer enter into a dialog where the marketer will learn a lot about the customer in order to better serve his or her needs, and the customer benefits by having his or her needs met in a semicustom fashion. This may often happen in a manner that is transparent to the customer, particularly on the Internet where emerging technologies exist that can combine, in real time, demographic data with purchasing feedback. These technologies allow the merchant to learn about the market and the individual in real time and to adjust the ad campaign and/or products being offered, immediately.

Regis McKenna [89] argues that marketers who continue to employ outdated marketing techniques—the blunderbuss approach of shouting and grabbing lapels—risk losing control of one of marketing's core values: the brand. The Web age has changed the brand experience from a one-way barrage of commercials instructing consumers which brand to buy without actually trying it out to brand preference developed as "an encapsulation of actual, experienced value. . . . Customer preferences expressed in dialog with producers or service providers—an exchange made possible by technology, and one in which the customer has the upper hand."

"How, in this environment, can companies create and maintain brand loyalty?" McKenna asks, and then gives the event-driven answer: "[A] rich dialog between producers and consumers. . . . That producer-customer interaction, made possible by the tools of the Information Age, will need to have its information systems tuned to real time if companies are to coordinate and deliver finely calibrated, timely responses to consumers."

Regis McKenna enumerates the characteristics of the "rich dialog" made possible by the event-driven "tools of the Information Age," all of which are enabled at the highest level by the event-driven architecture:

- Understand that consumers, given more control over what and how they buy through a dialog with companies, are, paradoxically, more open to being guided by those companies.

- "Analyze customer feedback constantly—with that feedback originating in many instances from customers closely tied to a company's operations."

- ■ "Act on that customer feedback, which calls for dynamic collaboration—based on shared information—between all of a company's departments and managerial functions."

- ■ "Closely monitor the quality and speed of a company's responsiveness to customer feedback."

- ■ Use new media—inside and outside the company— "allowing unprecedented subtle and nuanced human interaction."

- ■ Invest heavily in technologies that let customers satisfy themselves.

These last two points refer, of course, to the Internet, which completes the image of technology bringing the original marketer back to the original marketplace and promises a perfect setting for the intense interchanges of feedback, collaboration, and dialog that define markets of less than one. On the Internet, after all, goods and services are on display to hundreds of millions of people, one at a time. Given the Internet's potential for one-on-one interactivity, dialog between customers and marketers should be going on at full volume. But, as of this writing, it is not.

On a very simple level, the Internet allows for customer-supplier dialog, which results in product and service invention. But at most Web sites today, there's no option to link between the site and another form of communication with the company (most sites do not yet have a linking capability), and usually there is no possibility for a site for individual visitors. In most cases, a visitor to a Web site will see the exact same pages and exactly the same information, no matter how many times this visitor has been there before. It is like repeatedly meeting for the first time. This is why the corporate portal concept I discussed in Chapter 5 is so vital.

Don Peppers and Martha Rogers [90] commented on this issue in the March 12, 1998, edition of their weekly online newsletter:

> Most firms use their Web sites today to present what is essentially "brochureware," despite the fact that the Web itself is an inherently addressable, interactive medium. . . .

According to [research by] Palo Alto–based Shelley Taylor & Associates, sites actually tend to discourage direct contact with customers: only 37 percent of sites give customers company contact information; only 22 percent contain any post-sales information or support; and only 5 percent provide online support.

Web-based differentiation and personalization may be inevitable, but it hasn't happened yet—not on a large scale anyway. . . . Companies that recognize, early on, the value of individualized Web sites stand to gain a significant edge on their competitors.

Partners and Allies: Learning from Hollywood

The event-driven company looks very different from the contemporary company. It plays by newer rules. Organizationally the event-driven company is very much like a modern Hollywood movie studio. The studio provides basic infrastructure and then assembles an event-driven team—a director, a writer, a cinematographer, actors, technicians, and so on—for the specific purpose of producing a particular film to supersatisfy particular customers. Studios create value by adding something their customers want (entertainment) to a commoditized raw process (movie-making). Value exists in the eye of the customer. In the same manner, the event-driven company constantly creates value by deploying flexible, star-led teams that flock around value opportunities as they occur.

Similar to "ruthless" movie studios, which recognize few confining rules as they pursue their value-creating missions, event-driven companies have no patience with the conventional wisdom of contemporary organizations, including that pertaining to relationships with partners and allies. According to James Moore [91], "These . . . are businesses with an edge. In a sense, they are renegades. In their marauding ways, they do not respect traditional industry paradigms and partitions. Indeed, what they share is a tendency to upend business and industry models and to redraw increasingly porous boundaries."

Three pillars of conventional companies' partner and ally wisdom are the related concepts of supply-chain integration, the *keiretsu*, and the concept of the value chain. All are bedrock to the contemporary company and nearly irrelevant to the event-driven company.

Supply chain integration in the contemporary company, according to Raymond Miles [92], ". . . makes it difficult to determine where one organization ends and another begins" because of the "extension of . . . process backward and forward. . . . Suppliers are given access to large firms' scheduling and accounting processes. . . ." And so on. The *keiretsu* is an interlocked group of companies that do business primarily with one another, thereby discouraging the advances of outsiders.

The event-driven company has no use for permanently, or rigidly, integrated supply chains and the traditional *keiretsu*, because both are closed systems. Event-driven companies prefer more open systems, where the faces may not be familiar but where the rewards are greatest. In its January 17, 1998, edition, *The Economist* [93] magazine reports the rise of "old-fashioned cut-throat competition" in the new, Web-based economy that's replacing comfortable, closed arrangements such as the integrated supply chain. Under the headline, "Once Everyone Assumed Information Technology Would Bring Companies Together, Now It Threatens to Drive Them Apart," *The Economist* details the disintegration of the closed contemporary supply chain: "The Internet has turned the logic [of supply-chain integration] on its head. By using the Internet's technology, firms are beginning to use the Web to avoid their existing suppliers in search of ones that are faster and cheaper."

The Economist visits "online bazaars," where maverick suppliers, members of no one's supply chain or *keiretsu*, bid openly for contracts and seek out RFPs. Japan Airlines' Web site, for example, publishes specifications for such inflight commodities as plastic drinking cups, welcoming bids from any cup manufacturer that happens across the JAL site. JAL makes things easier for "outsiders" by posting downloadable versions of its logo and technical requirements for the cups, both of which were formerly proprietary materials.

In theory, supply-chain integration brings vendors and customers together as consultative partners instead of card-room adversaries, but in practice supply-chain integration often has more to do with accommodating mutual organizational deficiencies or the deficiencies of outmoded technology than with partnership and loyalty. Much of the networking along the integrated supply chain is the result of companies being handcuffed together with proprietary "electronic data interchange" (EDI) systems that communicate only with machines that speak the same private language.

The Economist cites the example of Boeing encouraging its suppliers to buy proprietary IT systems for the purpose of "slash[ing] the costs of processing orders and prevent[ing] logistical mishaps. Boeing put together a complete prototype of its 777 [this way]. . . . Before a single aircraft was built, Boeing and its suppliers ensured that every nut and bolt would fit into place."

But, notes *The Economist*: "The huge cost of these proprietary systems tended to oblige manufacturers to limit their suppliers, just as it obliged suppliers to concentrate on a few customers."

An event-driven company's systems are open, not proprietary, which invites competing players and allows the company to choose relationships anywhere in the ecosystem that create the best situational value for the event-driven company's customers. These choices are made on merit, not IT tyranny. Having been made with value uppermost in mind, and being forced to withstand the constant test of continuing value, such alliances create true loyalty.

While the event-driven company can switch suppliers in a heartbeat, it welcomes the possibility of being treated the same way by the companies it supplies. If a competitor can float into the picture and steal that customer, the event-driven company deserves to lose the business. Again, relationships that stand the test of ongoing value are much stronger than those forged by convenience, laziness, or habit.

LEADING THE CHANGE TO THE EVENT-DRIVEN COMPANY

Beating the Odds

Four out of five corporate change efforts in the United States fail, according to Douglas K. Smith [94]. Smith ascribes this dismal record to managers' inability to understand the underlying "behavior-driven" nature of such modern business revisions as TQM, BPR, and organizational learning. I agree completely. Managers attempting change institute new processes and new organizational ideas but often forget to motivate workers to understand the benefits of change and then to teach them *how* to change in concert with the new processes and ideas.

Overhauling the way a company does business calls for new skills and new relationships throughout the company's entire ecosystem—fundamentally new ways of looking at every process and every concept. Without generous portions of the right kind of leadership, workers will react to this avalanche of change as normal human beings—heading backward toward the "safety" of the way things were. You, the leader, might be a bit chary of change yourself, because change will rearrange the elements that brought you to your current eminence.

One might think that, because the change is rooted in technology, becoming event-driven is not quite the same as implementing BPR and TQM and other business revisions that appear to be about "ideas," not machines. But it is the same. To begin with, becoming event-driven is not an alternative to popular business change ideas. It's a way to make them work better. As with any radical change in your business structure and logic, becoming event-driven requires strong commitment to building a human infrastructure that matches and supports the new technology infrastructure that undergirds the ideas. While that's true of all business-change concepts, becoming event-driven is the only one that frankly acknowledges the primary role of technology as the engine that drives the realization of change. Even change efforts that are planned to be 20 percent technology and 80 percent culture turn out to be 80 percent technology.

Of course, different kinds of companies will require different kinds and amounts of change management depending on how much upheaval becoming event-driven generates. If a financial trader, for example, should one day find torrents of real-time, value-added, active information suddenly flowing to his or her workstation, that trader is going to leap at the chance to make more gravy instantly, before any *human* infrastructure changes are made or any motivational conversations have transpired. The best kind of management in this case is the kind that envisions and acquires the right technology and then jumps to safety to avoid the stampede. The financial trader, with his or her unique relationship with the machinery of profit creation, is likely to be an extremely early adopter of any event-driven change that becomes available.

On the other hand, different companies in the process of becoming event-driven might encounter the following situations:

- A procurement specialist confused by the new, wide-open, Internet-based nature of vendor selection

- A sales representative unsure how to handle his or her new authority to modify the factory's workflow

- A nascent star unsure of his or her abilities and new-found freedom

- A "do it my way" construction foreman frustrated by automated processes that require managing exceptions in a timely manner

- A workgroup director, accustomed to issuing status reports on his or her timetable, feeling undermined because this information is now published instantly to the entire organization the moment it becomes available

- Workers who have been "empowered" and managers tasked with doing that empowering without the confidence/experience to take advantage of the new opportunities

Becoming event-driven is far more than buying the right machines to link the right databases, knowledge resources, and computer applications. All the technology in the world won't help an organization's change-averse people become Warriors unless leaders inculcate the event-driven state of mind in the entire organization and demonstrate, by training and example, how that state of mind pays off in boosted customer value.

Let us clearly distinguish here between two concepts that are often used interchangeably: "leadership" and "management," "leaders" and "managers." "Managers" may be the worst people to lead a company's change. They've been successful until now keeping things moving the old way. Their charter is to make the organization hum smoothly. They thrive by *avoiding* urgency and the exceptional, making it harder for them to accept management by exception. They are, nearly by definition, heavily invested in the past.

Successful change does not require management; it requires leadership. A *manager* will stand off to one side and (fruitlessly) order workers to change the way they work. A *leader* will go first, becoming the pioneer who experiences changes his or her workers are being asked to make (whether those being led are 120,000 people in a global enterprise or a workgroup of five) and then use this experience to help guide workers through the transition. People cannot simply be ordered to change their behavior. In times of greatest upheaval, workers will draw enormous inspiration from *leaders* who share the journey, but will ignore, even undermine, *managers* who issue orders from the sidelines.

The quality of top leadership may well determine the success or failure of becoming event-driven. As Don Peppers and Martha Rogers [95] point out, "There are many reasons your firm's culture will block the way [to change], but there is only one reason it might not: you."

If you're doing business in the world today, you are short of time. That's good. A leader becoming event-driven should not waste breath explaining the rationale for change. If your colleagues have their wits about them—which they must, or they wouldn't be your colleagues—they already know *why* the company has to change. What they want to know is how it will change, what the change will mean to them, how they can do their part, and how everyone in the company's ecosphere will benefit from the change.

Leadership: Beyond Charisma

A company's transition to event-driven is best served by a form of evolving, shape-shifting leadership that is compelling and visionary in the chrysalis stage and then becomes increasingly educational and inspirationally coach-like as the event-driven culture takes hold. The formula reminds me of dissolving sutures used by oral surgeons; these hold the tissues firmly together until the body is strong enough to take over the healing process and then, having done their job, melt away.

In a monograph on "Leadership and Organizational Changes" in the *California Management Review*, David A. Nadler and Michael L. Tushman [96] echo this concept, discussing the evolution of change leadership from "charismatic" to "instrumental." The successful charismatic leader *envisions* and then articulates a future—exciting and credible—with which workers can identify and around which they can rally.

The next step is *energizing*—a series of demonstrations of enthusiasm that motivate workers to act toward achieving the vision. Energizing can be the mere exhibition of excitement or one-on-one conversations struck up during management by walking around.

In the next stage, *enabling,* "the leader psychologically helps people act or perform in the face of challenging goals, [displaying] the ability to listen, understand, and share the feelings of those in the organization . . . express support for individuals . . . express his or her confidence in people's ability to perform effectively to meet challenges."

Once change is launched, charismatic leadership becomes a double-edged sword. The visionary energy that got everybody fired up may now raise expectations to unreasonable levels: Members of the organization may expect too much too soon from the change, and the leader may be expected to continue generating continuous "magic." If things don't work out exactly as promised, workers will feel betrayed. A cult of personality may develop, in which people look to the charismatic leader alone for approval and leadership, thus disenfranchising other leaders and making it harder for the star system to emerge.

Since the charismatic leader worked hard at convincing everyone to change, disagreement with him or her may become more difficult to sustain. Finally, a charismatic leader lights the fire of change, but may lack execution skills to keep the fire burning in the everyday business of the organization.

As many start-up companies know, there comes a moment after the giddy months of organization and successful launch when people look at one another and say, in effect, "Holy Toledo! We're actually in business. Now what?" The same feeling may permeate an organization that has installed the event-driven infrastructure and now finds enormous amounts of active information flowing to its people. Now what?

Now is the moment that calls for leaders to ensure that the company's structure and processes are optimized to contribute most effectively to achieving the vision bequeathed by the charismatics. The leader encourages and organizes the flocking of teams around the company's objectives, codifies the range of best practices, develops systems to quantify results, and conceives and executes the most efficacious ways to dole out incentives (and disincentives) to encourage workers to behave in ways that move them and the company toward creation of amplified customer value.

One thing to watch out for at this stage is a form of technological "rapture of the depths." Key technology users within an organization can get so caught up in event-driven capabilities that they forget to design appropriate processes and systems to make the most of their new information nirvana. Having the capability to push real-time, active information throughout an organization's ecosphere via publish/subscribe, for example, means nothing unless a company designs useful subscription lists and determines who should get what information, why, and in what form.

Becoming so enraptured with event-driven capabilities that one fails to invent and then implement proper processes to exploit those capabilities violates Caveat Number 1 of the change to event-driven: Becoming event-driven is not a magic bullet. Becoming event-driven doesn't improve poor processes, add quality to bad applications, make up for a lack of useful information in a company, or create valuable content where none existed before. Becoming event-driven is an amplifier for good companies, not a cure for bad companies. It will make good companies work better and bad companies discover their failures more quickly.

Missionaries

The charismatic leader finds people within the organization who are eager to change and from them recruits what Don Peppers and Martha Rogers [97] call "missionaries"—customer value creators at all levels, from the grass roots to the executive suite—to act as agents modeling the processes and concomitant benefits of change. Despite their "special" status as missionaries, these shock troops should work within the company's existing structure: It's a bad idea to set up a separate group that could become another bureaucracy down the road. Missionaries commit to repeating the mantra of change as often as possible. There is no such thing as too much repetition. Just when a missionary is about to get sick from repeating the message so often, someone somewhere in the company is just beginning to get it. The leader and the missionaries strive constantly to expand the circle of people taking responsibility for the process of becoming event-driven.

The "here's how we do it" stage is equally vital. Explain, explain, explain. Explain to each person how his or her function matters to the company. If the event-driven infrastructure puts new emphasis on cross-functional teams, teach team-building skills. If the company is amping up its customer focus, as it should, develop and promulgate systems that base job evaluation, compensation, and bonus on the creation of customer value. If leaders are being asked to find ways to let their workers empower themselves and workers are being asked to assume more responsibility at the customer interface, both groups must be taught exactly how to go about it. Put more emphasis on the work people do, not the orders they're allowed to give. Extol improvisation and the ability to learn and teach from failure.

The most effective leadership for a company becoming event-driven will start out charismatic and then shift to instrumental. The legacy of charismatic leadership will prove valuable during the transition to instrumental. The charismatic leader's "envisioning" becomes the company's vision, which, once established independently of the leader, permanently mitigates against anything that disempowers workers. If the vision is established, respected, and raised high so that it's clearly visible to all, everyone knows where the company is going and workers needn't check with *The Boss* or a boss before acting.

While the charismatic leader often relies on a few grand gestures to rally and inspire the troops, the instrumental leader is anchored in day-to-day events that make up the experience known as "doing business." Fortunately, the event-driven infrastructure gives leaders a great tool to execute their jobs day after day—the executive information system (EIS) or a portal customized for leaders. Similar in physical appearance to the financial trader's MarketSheet, the event-driven EIS is configured to present moment-to-moment, cross-section snapshots of the organization. Traditional EISs rely on passive data collected from the systems throughout the company. The EIS allows one to see the business from a summary level, or to "drill down" into more detail as desired. With an event-driven IT infrastructure, the EIS becomes something much more dynamic, because some or all of the data are real time. Instead of sifting through history, the executive now monitors what is happening as it happens. Historical analysis still has its place, of course, but combined with active information, the EIS is able to provide a complete picture of the past and the present. This picture allows the leader to monitor and access the effects of change as they happen, allowing real-time adjustments in the communications with the organization.

Overcoming Barriers to Change

Organizational resistance to change is, of course, not unique to companies becoming event-driven, although initial discomfort may be stronger than usual for the simple reason that becoming event-driven means an extensive revamping of processes and the way of doing business. A colleague who has overseen a Fortune 100 company's transition to event-driven characterizes the negative internal reaction he'd hear from workers in the way many objected to the new and much more efficient technology of automobiles in the early twentieth century: "I used to ride my bicycle just fine. I don't want to learn to drive a car, with its complicated windshield wipers and headlights and unnecessarily complex controls. I get where I need to go just fine as it is." Indeed, you can get there on a bicycle, but think how infinitely more efficient a car is!

Until a company becomes event-driven, its processes, as well as its applications and databases, are disconnected islands, and each island has its own indigenous culture, with its own chiefs. Becoming event-driven unites the islands, forcing the indigenous cultures to blend and disenfranchising the chiefs of fiefdoms. Information, once the tightly guarded treasure of each island leader, now circulates freely. In one company that became event-driven, a department manager complained bitterly that every decision his department made was instantly published to the whole company. He felt threatened by the publication of "his" information to others in the company and worried that he might occasionally "look bad" if his department's activities were automatically shared with the rest of the organization.

Initial resistance and confusion are not surprising. Operating in the event-driven environment is not necessarily more complex, although it is natural for something new to feel complex. What workers were used to was a request/reply model of obtaining information that they had complete control over, and now information comes coursing onto their desks via real-time infrastructure software.

Some workers, put off by the more challenging new environment, are tempted to point out what's wrong with becoming event-driven rather than anticipating the benefits once new complexity is mastered. Leadership must play a role in inspiring people to change, explaining the superior value of change—to customers and to workers—and patiently educating workers how to thrive in the new environment. Leaders must also walk employees through an adjustment period, during which all of the kinks have not been worked out of the system yet. Despite everyone's best efforts, there is a transition period for both workers and the system, and everybody needs to be patient and willing to learn, because, after all, the change is for the better.

There are, of course, also incredibly positive initial responses to a company's event-driven transition. Many workers perceive the benefits to becoming event-driven from the start and recognize that everything that once required such enormous time and labor is now being done so swiftly and automatically—and accurately. There is often a tendency to want to verify that things are working correctly: It can't be that easy. They often want to stop the event-driven process and examine the system for the errors they are certain such speed must create. As more companies employ the event-driven infrastructure to achieve real-time, "straight-through processing" of business transactions, there is less need for information to stop at traditional bureaucratic borders for reworking. This hands-off speed makes some workers uneasy.

Financial traders in the 1980s found it hard at first to believe that one screen could present all the incoming information that they'd previously harvested laboriously from 25 different sources on a dozen different screens. They were hard put to believe that the outgoing information they generated—reports on securities sales, for example—was also being handled automatically instead of requiring the painstaking, by-hand data entry to which they were accustomed. Today, workers in some of the world's largest banks are also impressed the first time back-office, middle-office, and front-office applications talk to one another in real time, clearing complex transactions instantly and eliminating the need for laborious transfers of information and repetitive rekeying of data.

The workers who will become stars in the new, event-driven environment are those who most quickly understand that the event-driven infrastructure doesn't rob people of meaningful work; rather, it relieves them of low-value tasks and empowers their personal execution by exception. The transition to event-driven is a transition from a labor-intensive, information-starved model to one that renders everyone in the company a knowledge worker.

The most reassuring and effective message that leaders can broadcast is that once the organization becomes event-driven, everything that machines can handle will actually be handled by machines (because the event-driven architecture maximizes automated capabilities). Everything a person is asked to do, therefore, is exceptional and requires exceptional knowledge and reasoning skills. And *you* are the people being asked to do it!

CHAPTER **10**
CONCLUSION

The Age of the Knowledge Worker

Depending on when you read this book, the thoughts and views about the future of global commerce and the advantageous deployment of integrated, active business information are going to seem:

- Like some far-fetched fantasy
- On the cutting edge
- What everybody is saying these days
- What everybody has known all along

In other words, what may seem far-fetched in 1999 will be general reality in a few Internet minutes. I'm convinced that, with the passage of time, everything I've said in this book is only going to become more relevant to the business executive dedicated to outpacing galloping commoditization by finding an enduring competitive advantage.

When I first sketch the benefits of the event-driven infrastructure to new business acquaintances, many indeed think the concept is a fantasy. Their experience is that tying just two applications, two databases, or two corporate subsidiaries together is challenging enough. To them it seems like a distant and impossibly complex dream to link an enterprise's entire flow of information, from any number of sources, in a manner that gathers, integrates, and upgrades internally and externally generated information and delivers it to the people who need it, all in real time.

But it is not a future dream. It can be done today. It must be done soon: The need for globally integrated, real-time, information-delivery systems is already clearly apparent as I write this (in the summer of 1999) and will only become more so as the networked world spins ever closer to reality.

The launch of low-earth-orbit satellite systems within the next few years will make ours a completely wired planet webbed by networks of networks that will, together, form a metanetwork on which all of us will communicate and do business. This metanetwork will enable the fluid business alliances I propose in this book as an open-systems replacement for the limited supply chain and facilitate the complete integration of enterprise information systems, no matter how geographically distant the companies are from one another. The "universal translator" element of the event-driven infrastructure will make communication possible between and among systems once they're linked via the network.

We'll use the network, as well, to manage the details of our daily existence. Business leaders and pundits in the technology industry all refer to the imminent emergence of a new generation of network "appliances" that will allow network access without a PC. These appliances range from highly functional phones to two-way paging devices and include a new generation of network-aware home appliances (in the conventional sense of the word). The day is almost here when you'll be able to phone home (or use the functions on your mobile phone) to order your air conditioner to cool the premises to 72 degrees by 6:00 P.M. and have coffee ready for you at 7:00 A.M. the next morning. Soon everything will be connected to the metanetwork, from the most mission-critical applications on your company's server computers to the hot-water sensor in your shower. This may seem extreme, but imagine the gains in both freedom and control if virtually every device at home or work can be accessed through the network and configured to suit the service you're using at the time. Everything becomes accessible from everything and from anywhere. In an event-driven world this ubiquitous access is extended further, since reports and repercussions of every "event" will ripple through the network—analyzed, acted upon, and delivered where they are needed. The extensions of this concept are fascinating. It starts with the very simple, when, for example, your "smart" microwave oven allows you to start dinner on your way home, and extends to include hand-held multimedia devices, which download the appropriate software and configure themselves to be a video phone or an interactive game, depending on your requirements of the moment.

The ubiquity of the network brings with it ubiquity of information, and that development has profound implications for the way people will work. Because real-time information integration is now possible, there will be almost no need for workers who engage in the type of commodity work the Institute for the Future [98] calls "the mindless capturing, recording, and moving around [of] information and data." Instead, nearly everyone who holds a white-collar job will be a value-added knowledge worker of some sort. Calling employed people "knowledge workers" is by no means the same as calling janitors "sanitation engineers." The appellation truly describes what these people do: add value to their work product . . . or be replaced by ever-smarter machines.

There is, of course, a tremendous difference between data and information and knowledge. Data and information are the ore, knowledge the refined end product. The refining process is a combination of applied human and mechanical abilities. Humans bring to bear their creativity, intuition, passion, experience, drive, and luck, among other characteristics. Ordinary machines can provide analysis, gargantuan memory, global reporting capabilities, and real-time speed. Event-driven information technology can provide that and much more.

The event-driven company will, as I have said, develop both the human and technological infrastructures to refine data and information into knowledge that can elevate the company above rust—that is, commoditization—and the competition. In the event-driven organization, the business ecosphere's total information universe is delivered in real time to well-compensated, well-motivated, customer-focused, highly talented "stars" for refinement into knowledge and superior customer value. No matter the diversity of information sources, no matter the machine language in which the information is written, no matter the location of the information source or the worker who needs to know, the event-driven infrastructure normalizes and enriches the information and then serves it up to people for the final process of refinement into knowledge. Employees on the receiving end of event-driven information are, by the very nature of the "ore" they receive, knowledge workers.

The Digital Age is already creating strong demand for knowledge workers—a demand that will only grow as we enter the era of the global network. According to a recent study by Anthony Carnevale and Stephen Rose [99], economists at the Educational Testing Service, the strongest current demand for workers is not in science and information technology, as one would suppose, but for what I believe is a new type of knowledge-centric office worker. A full 40 percent of all employed Americans now work in offices. Some are no doubt doing the routine work of moving data around and will soon be rendered redundant by event-driven information systems. But millions of other office workers are representative of the new generation of knowledge workers.

Compared with 15 years ago, a far greater proportion of today's office workers are professionals, and far fewer hold such support jobs as secretary. More than half of the new office workers have at least a bachelor's degree. They include managers and executives; communications and financial experts; marketers; business consultants; lawyers; high-level sales people, such as real estate and stock brokers; and scientists and engineers, who work in management rather than in the classroom or the lab.

In my view, many of these "office workers" are knowledge workers filling new types of jobs–which just happen to be in offices–created by the automated technologies that destroyed the old, routine jobs. Anthony Carnevale and Stephan Rose [100] report that of America's 52 million office workers, nearly 10 million are managers; another 4 million are management professionals, such as accountants; and another 4 million are sales people and brokers in real estate, finance, and insurance. About 1.5 million are science-based professionals, such as engineers, architects, and chemists, who also work in an office. That's 20 million knowledge workers, and their era is just beginning.

Writing in the *New York Review of Books*, Jeff Mardick [101] recently suggested that the new office workers "seem to supply the ideas that, in . . . the modern economy are in ever greater demand. . . . [E]ducated office workers appear to be the source of business innovations, which include an increasingly rapid flow of new products and services, ad campaigns, marketing concepts, financing techniques, and managerial reforms."

This new class of knowledge worker was made possible by the rise of technology that, in effect, shuffles paper automatically. The new knowledge worker (and his or her company) realizes that the value humans can add to automated information—especially in an event-driven system—becomes more narrowly defined as the quality of the automated information increases. Out go the paper shufflers, in come the value-added knowledge workers.

The meaning of "paper shuffler" keeps inching up the skill ladder as automation gets "smarter." Increased machine intelligence is being made possible by the late-1990s comeback of artificial intelligence (AI), which were written off as over-hyped "solutions without problems" in the 1970s. These AI systems can do many things people can. They might even replace members of the Warrior class: You may recall the financial services CEO who told me he was going to replace eight of his ten top traders, who earned bonuses that averaged $5 million a year, with a sophisticated, AI-based, event-driven trading system. He'll keep his top two traders to handle the most exceptional situations and motivate them with $10 million bonuses, thus saving an annual $30 million.

Event-driven IT systems shuffle paper better than it's ever been shuffled before, but they don't threaten to put truly talented people out of work. Just the opposite: Relieved of "tasks even a machine could do," people can turn to the greater challenge and satisfaction of Jeff Mardick's [102] "business innovations: an increasingly rapid flow of new products and services, ad campaigns, marketing concepts, financing techniques, and managerial reforms." As the reader will have gleaned from preceding chapters, the event-driven company, by its nature, creates demand and provides tools for precisely these human-generated programs. They are the natural outgrowth of the event-driven company's intense communication with customers, its culture of product and service invention to solve customers' problems, its ability to recognize and track changes within its customer base in real time, and its dedication to reshaping management to support customer-obsessed stars.

How Becoming Event-Driven Can Spur Your Company's Productivity

One of the more puzzling and most discussed conundrums of the Digital Age is that the productivity of American workers has not blasted upward in tandem with the introduction of evermore sophisticated information technologies. Although there may have been a slight uptick in productivity in the late 1990s, the pace of productivity growth since the 1970s has been sluggish compared with the previous decades.

I'm not a professional economist, so my opinion is just that, but if one looks at the periods in recent history during which productivity increased most rapidly, one common element is that during those periods technology turned certain jobs into commodities, thus driving people out of the production process. This is not a cold-hearted statement. Social-welfare advocates during the Industrial Revolution worried that mass production would create an entire class of permanently impoverished former workers, but what happened instead was that the prosperity created by mass production spurred development of new industries that eagerly hired displaced workers at better wages and gave them more interesting jobs.

Nearly a century later, we are witnessing an echo of the same process, as information technology puts people out of commodity work. No tragedy: Who wants to do work a machine can do better and faster? There's little challenge in that. And, once again, the prosperity of the Digital Age is spurring the creation of new industries that can't find enough workers to hire. Though job creation is consuming most workers being displaced by new technology, same as the old days, what's different this time is that worker productivity is not increasing rapidly the way it did during earlier periods of widespread automation, including the rise of mass production in the late nineteenth and early twentieth centuries and the mad postwar boom of the 1950s and 1960s.

The reason productivity is lagging in the Digital Age may be that the original wave of technology created *mass* production, whereas today's IT revolution is creating *customized* production. Mass production requires little human creativity; customized production nothing but. In his *New York Review of Books* article, Jeff Mardick [103] argues, "[T]he new economy may simply not be able to remove human beings from the production process as rapidly as the old standardized economy of the mass production age. . . . [I]t is worth exploring whether the growing need for human imagination might inevitably hold back [productivity's] rate of growth."

One great beauty of the event-driven infrastructure is that it enables true, customer-pleasing *mass customization*, a combination that, on one hand, relieves the maximum number of people from "mindless" commodity work (à la mass production) while, on the other hand, amplifying the importance of human creativity (à la customized production) without slowing production processes. If anything, event-driven production moves even more quickly than before. What's more, companies experience a benefit on a micro level that the macro economy experienced during times of great technological advances: People thrown out of commodity work create new, higher-value industries; but in the event-driven universe, they do it inside the company's structure.

I have done no studies to support this claim, but I conclude from experience with customers that converting a company to event-driven tends to increase its productivity at a rate comparable to or greater than historical periods of greatest productivity growth in the larger economy.

The New Meaning of Life/Workspace

Event-driven infrastructures will free people from commodity work at the same time they provide far more engaging work environments. The quality of workers will soon be so high that inviting *digital* work environments will become as much a recruiting inducement as inviting *physical* workspaces. To attract and keep stars of highest magnitude, and to draw from them their greatest value-creating effort, companies will be obliged to make work more like an adventure or a game. Grafting exciting user interfaces onto the flow of active information, event-driven systems will present sales reports, for example, as fly-through, 3-D landscapes that reflect real-time sales activity. (See that purple mountain rising and falling over there? That's the foot traffic in our northeastern stores.) Creative user interfaces will tap directly into people's desires to compete and win, framing information flow as a strategic projection of their companies' strategies and processes.

One outgrowth will be even less distinction between the times we're "working" and the times we're enjoying leisure. This path has two possible end points: an exaggeration of what we have today, in which many people are, in effect, manacled to work by their technological leashes (pagers, cell phones, etc.), and a far more pleasant alternate destination in which work, stripped by machines of all but its creative content, will become as exciting and stimulating as any book or movie. And each person will be a star performer in the continuing saga of his or her life/work.

The Event-Driven Future

This book has been a combination of explanation and exhortation, attempting to explain how the event-driven architecture's new way of treating information gives rise to an entirely new way of doing business, and exhorting readers to embrace the future as soon as possible.

As our life/workspace converges, the event-driven architecture may improve the future quality not just of our companies but of our very lives. Until quite recently, we as a technological society were good at generating ever-greater quantities of information, but not so good at making sense of it. Most people, when asked, will tell you there is far more information out there today than they care to handle. It pounds on their doors, comes in through the telephone lines, jumps at them from their TVs and monitors, blathers in airports and elevators, and lands on their front steps with a thud each morning.

The event-driven architecture is designed to get control of this torrent, no matter how copious, organize and make sense of all the information arriving from a variety of sources, and then bring you what you want to know, what you need to know, and what you ought to know to live and work with greater value.

GLOSSARY

ACL (Access Control List)—A list that tells computers and systems which access rights individual users have. A method of permissioning access to information resources within an organization.

ActiveX—Microsoft technology that adds enhancements to OLE to allow software components to be distributed across networks and integrated into Web browsers.

Agent—A software component that stands in for a user or for another program and prepares and exchanges information or takes action on its behalf.

AI (Artificial Intelligence)—The field of computer science that attempts to model human thought onto computer behavior.

amazoned—Having your traditional business rapidly surpassed by an Internet start-up (i.e., "we got amazoned.")

API (Application Program Interface)—An interface to access the operating system or other services. The API lets developers create code to interface with a given application or program.

Applet—A small Java program that can be embedded in an HTML page as a sort of miniprogram for animation or computational tasks.

Application adapters—Software used to connect applications to a messaging system. Adapters ensure that the external application behaves as if it were native to the messaging environment.

Application architecture—The structure of components in an application system.

Authenticator—A data object that authenticates an identity. Data security programs use two kinds of authenticators: certificates and tokens.

Avatar—A virtual identity assumed by visitors on the Internet, in a virtual reality world or chat room.

B2B (Business-to-Business)—Used to describe transactions where one business sells to another business (rather than directly to consumers).

B2C (Business-to-Consumer)—Used to describe transactions where a business sells directly (or through channels) to the end user/consumer.

Backbone—A high-speed line or series of connections that forms a major pathway within a network.

Back end system—Software that performs the core functions of the enterprise.

Bandwidth—The maximum amount of data that can be transmitted through a physical network connection, typically measured in bits per second.

Batch processing—A system that runs a set of commands or tasks automatically without human intervention often on a daily or weekly basis or as system resources become available. Allows completion of a set of tasks as a single group.

BPR (Business Process Reengineering)—A consulting strategy that focuses on altering the processes of business for increased efficiencies.

Broadband—A transmission system that multiplexes multiple independent signals onto one cable. In telecommunication technology, any channel having a bandwidth greater than a voice-grade channel (4 kHz). In LAN technology, a coaxial cable on which analog signaling is used.

Business object—A software object that contains the data and the logic relating to a business abstraction, such as an order, or a software object representing an event of interest to an enterprise, such as a change to an order or stock price.

Cash-to-cash—The cycle time between cash cost outlays for production/development and cash received for products sold.

CICS (Customer Information Control System)—An online transaction processing program (OLTP) from IBM. Combined with the COBOL language, CICS has become one of the most common sets of tools for creating customer transaction systems.

Clicks—When a visitor clicks on a banner ad to go to the advertiser's Web site, it is counted as a click or "click through" by ad buyers and sellers.

Client/server architecture—A system for information processing in which clients (programs or users) request tasks from other systems (servers) and wait for a response.

COM (Common Object Model)—A software architecture from Microsoft that allows applications to be built from software components.

Competitive flexibility—The ability to react quickly to new market opportunities and challenges and profit from them as they occur.

Component architecture—A programming methodology that allows applications to be built from generic, reusable building blocks (components).

Cookie—Information placed on a user's hard drive by Web sites to uniquely identify the user across multiple visits, allowing for the evaluation of user activity.

CORBA (Common Object Request Broker Architecture)—A standard programming specification based on OMG (Object Management Group) standards that defines the interface between OMG-compliant objects.

Core competencies—What you or your company does best.

CPM (Cost Per Mille)—The rate used by Internet and sellers and buyers. The CPM is the cost per thousand page views of a given banner ad.

CRM (Customer Relationship Management)—A methodology and software for managing customer relationships. It could include a database for the sales force, executives, and customer service representatives that describes details about customer needs and history and that provides the ability to match these criteria with a company's products ad service offerings. Often refers to systems that work with/over the Internet.

Cross-platform—Any language, software program, application, or device that works on multiple platforms.

DARPA (Defense Advanced Research Project Agency)—Part of the U.S. Department of Defense dedicated to the research and development of military defense systems and responsible for creating DARPAnet in the late 1960s, the precursor of today's Internet.

Data mining—A term that refers to analyzing data in a database or databases based on patterns and anomalies.

Data warehousing—A process by which stored data are extracted from production databases and conventional files and placed in a separate database for analytical purposes.

DBMS (Database Management System)—A set of programs to manage the organization and storage of data, as well as queries of that data by many users. A DBMS can manage security as well.

DCOM (Distributed Component Object Model)—A protocol that enables Microsoft COM-based software components to communicate over a network.

Decrypt—To restore the original content of an encrypted message. Used for e-commerce or security purposes.

Demand-driven—The opposite of event-driven. A demand-driven architecture performs tasks when asked by users or another program.

Dial-up—The point-to-point connection made over regular telephone lines to standard communication modems. Generally uses PPP.

Digital signature—Derived data that authenticate a document's or message's content and origin.

Distributed application—An application in which component programs are distributed across two or more computers on a network.

Distributed system—Data processing in which distributed applications cooperate.

Domain name—The unique name that identifies an Internet site. Domain names always have two or more parts, separated by dots. A given machine may have more than one domain name, but a given domain name points to only one machine.

EAI (Enterprise Application Integration)—The connection of existing islands of function (applications) into end-to-end flows with minimal impact on those islands.

EBI (Enterprise Business Integration)—The development of business process flows on top of the EAI infrastructure that deal with the entire enterprise as a set of virtual business processes that span multiple physical systems, networks, operating systems, and so on.

E-Commerce (Electronic Commerce)—Commerce activities conducted through electronic, or digital, means. Generally refers to any commerce conducted over the Internet or private computer networks.

E-Corporation—A company that has integrated its core business systems and processes into one seamless flow of information, and extended the reach of its business over the Internet to share information with customers, partners, and suppliers.

EDI (Electronic Data Interchange)—The exchange of data in the form of standardized documents over networks for business use.

EIP (Enterprise Information Portal)—A portal used to aggregate and organize the content and services of an enterprise, as well as external content for use by its employees, customers, and business partners.

EIS (Executive Information System)—A visualization tool for making the information of the enterprise visible to those who need it.

EJB (Enterprise Java Beans)—A software architecture from Sun that allows distributed applications to be built from software components.

E-Mail (Electronic Mail)—A method for sending messages and information to other users over computer networks (including the Internet).

Encryption—A method for securing data to prevent unauthorized access or forgery.

End point—The destination of a message, denoted by either an in-box name or a subject name.

ERP (Enterprise Resource Planning)—An accounting-type system and application used for planning and accounting of an enterprise's resources. Includes shipping, order management, accounting, and so on.

Event—A business object or other item of interest to a company such as an order or a stock price change.

Event-driven—A process by which an information system, infrastructure, or company responds to events (new or changing information), creating a flow of information throughout the system that accomplishes a desired outcome. For example, if a customer places an order, an event-driven system will carry the fulfillment of that order through the ordering, shipping, accounting, and billing processes.

Eyeballs—The number of people or eyeballs that visit your Web site or portal. In the age of the Internet the battle is for increased eyeballs.

Firewall—Hardware or software that serves as a buffer between any connected public network and a private network. A firewall uses access lists and other methods to control access to the private network and ensure security.

FTP (File Transfer Protocol)—A method for downloading files to and from an Internet site.

GUI (Graphical User Interface)—A program that uses graphics (images, buttons, clickable items, and so on) to present information and application functions to the user. Examples include Microsoft Windows operating system and popular Web browsers and the Internet.

Hits—The number of viewers who access a particular Web site/Web page.

HTML (HyperText Markup Language)—A coding language used to create pages on the World Wide Web. HTML files can link to any other documents on the Web. Documents can be viewed through a browser.

HTTP (HyperText Transfer Protocol)—The protocol for moving hypertext files on the Internet. The most important protocol used in the World Wide Web (WWW).

Information management—The management of the information resources of a company or organization, including information technology and other issues related to how information is accessed and distributed throughout an enterprise.

Internet—A global network linking computers of all types on a common underlying protocol called IP (Internet Protocol).

Internet backbone—High-speed networks that carry the Internet's traffic.

Intranet—A private network inside a company or organization that typically uses the same kinds of software you would find on the public Internet (e.g., browsers, HTML, etc.), but that is secured for internal use.

IP (Internet Protocol)—A set of standards for data transmission over the Internet.

IP address—A unique number that identifies every computer on the Internet.

ISDN (Integrated Service Digital Network)—Communication protocol, offered by telephone companies, that permits telephone networks to carry data, voice, and other source traffic.

ISP (Internet Service Provider)—A company that provides individuals and/or businesses with Internet access.

Java—A network-oriented programming language invented by Sun Microsystems that is designed for writing programs that can be downloaded to your computer over the Internet and immediately run.

JavaBeans—Component architecture for Java, allows for reusable software components, which can be assembled and contextualized to build applications.

Jini—Sun's extension of Java to enable communication between all types of computing devices over a network to allow for easy access to information and services.

Keizan teian—A Japanese term that refers to a continuous upgrade loop process (as found in event-driven systems).

LAN (Local Area Network)—A geographically limited network of computers/systems. Usually in one building.

LDAP (Lightweight Directory Access Protocol)—A software protocol for enabling people to locate organizations, individuals, and resources in a network, over the Internet, or on a corporate intranet. LDAP allows you to search for an individual or a resource without knowing their domain name (where they are located).

Legacy system—A term used to refer to older or custom systems that are often costly and difficult to replace and that present challenges when trying to integrate them with newer, more standardized systems in the enterprise.

Load balancing—A strategy for sending requests to the most available servers within a system to maximize throughput.

Manage by exception—The process of automating routine tasks so that the majority of a company's business process is handled electronically, allowing humans to focus on where the most risk and reward lie in the exceptions. Event-driven systems can identify exceptions, bringing them to the attention of the appropriate individuals, so that a company can avoid risky mistakes and fully take advantage of opportunities.

MBONE (Multicast backBONE)—A network that sits on top of the Internet and allows multicasting of data, video, and audio. Permits video conferencing over the Internet and streaming video.

Message transformation—A process for transforming the content of a message from one predefined format into another predefined format automatically. Allows for information exchange between diverse applications.

Messaging—The fundamental layer of the event-driven enterprise, messaging is the transport for all information exchanged among applications.

Metadata—Literally, information about data. The "description of the form" that contains the data.

Middleware—Software that connects the systems in an enterprise together so that they can share data. Allows distributed computing across heterogeneous computing platforms. Central to becoming event-driven.

Mosaic—The first Web browser that essentially made the World Wide Web accessible to the general public for the first time.

Multicast—A protocol that sends a single packet from one machine to a specific subset of network addresses. When compared to sending a copy of the same message to each individual network address (unicast), the ability to multicast a single copy conserves bandwidth and increases scalability.

NAP (Network Access Point)—A connection to the Internet backbone network.

Network—Two or more computers connected so that they can transfer/exchange data.

Object—In an object-oriented model, an object contains both the data and the logic that relates to a specific abstraction as defined by its class.

OLTP (OnLine Transaction Processing)—A program that manages transaction-oriented applications used for data entry and query transactions. OLTPs are used in most industries for online interactions/transactions with customers.

Online Service Provider—A paid service (such as CompuServe or America Online) that provides services and content to subscribers beyond simple Internet access. Services such as chat rooms, newsgroups, shopping networks, and so on are offered.

ORB (Object Request Broker)—Programming that acts as a "broker" between a client request for a service from a distributed object or component and the completion of that request. By using an ORB a client program can request a service without having to understand where the server is in a distributed network. Components can find out about each other and exchange interface information as they are running.

OS (Operating System)—Software that tells a computer how to perform basic functions such as saving files or accessing external devices attached to the computer.

Page views—The number of viewers a particular page on the Internet receives. A measure to determine advertising rates and traffic.

PDA (Personal Digital Assistant)—A hand-held computer device used for keeping notes, address books, appointments, and so on. Includes the Palm Pilot and Windows CE devices.

PGM (Pragmatic General Multicast)—An emerging reliable multicast protocol standard developed by Cisco and TIBCO in collaboration.

Plug and play—Describes systems, applications, or devices that can be plugged in and immediately played—no configuration is necessary.

Point-to-point message—A message addressed to a single destination.

Poll—To periodically request information from a server, usually to detect if there has been a change to some information on the server. In contrast, in and event-driven architecture, the server would generate an event when such a change occurs and polling would not be necessary.

Portal—A gateway to a collection of information and online services that provides a single organizational scheme and access point. Portals can be consumer-oriented, as in the case of Yahoo! or Netscape, or targeted to a specific audience, as is the case with an Enterprise Information Portal (EIP) that provides access to external and internal corporate content.

PPP (Point-to-Point Protocol)—The communication protocol generally used over telephone lines for modem connections.

Process flow control—A system/logic for capturing the rules of the enterprise that govern how various types of information flow among processes.

Protocol—Formal description of a set of rules and conventions that govern how devices on a network exchange information.

Publish/subscribe—Refers to technology that can instantly and automatically publish (deliver) to everyone in the environment the information that they need (subscribe to). Publish/subscribe technology is one of the technology cornerstones of the event-driven enterprise, allowing efficient real-time distribution of information over public or private networks (including the Internet).

Pull—Synonymous with request/reply. Asking for information rather than having it published to your attention.

Push—Real "push" is publish/subscribe. Information you want (subscribe to) is pushed to you in real time, as it happens.

QoS (Quality of Service)—The idea that messages may have different priorities, guarantees of delivery, security, and so on—that is, different "Qualities of Service." On the Internet and in other networks, QoS (Quality of Service) is the idea that these characteristics can be measured, improved, and, to some extent, guaranteed in advance. QoS is of particular concern for video and multimedia content.

Real time—Something that is done/delivered as it happens. Could refer to the posting of information about a stock trade as it happens, confirmation that a computer you have ordered will be shipped on a given date as it is booked, and so on. Immediate.

Reliable multicast—A protocol that runs on top of standard IP Multicast for reliable delivery of multicast packets across a network. (*See also* PGM.)

Request/reply—Refers to technology where a user/client application obtains information only when it is asked for. For example, to see if the information on a stock quote has changed, in a request/reply paradigm, a trader would have to constantly query a database for an update. With event-driven or publish/subscribe technology infrastructures, however, that information is automatically sent to the trader (without the trader having to request it) the moment it updates.

Router—A network layer device that uses one or more metrics to determine the optimal path along which network traffic should be forwarded. Routers forward packets from one network to another based on network layer information.

Search engine—A program that allows you to search by keyword for content on the Internet or in databases or file systems.

Server—A computer or software package whose services are used by users running on other computers. Examples include Web and e-mail servers. Usually implies a point-to-point, request/reply communication.

SSL (Secure Sockets Layer) —A public security protocol that creates a secure link between two applications, most commonly a Web browser and server.

Stickiness—A descriptive term for a Web site or portal that users can't stay away from because it is so good, useful, or compelling.

Streaming—A method for playing a video or audio files in real time instead of having to download the entire file.

Subject-based addressing—A message-addressing technique that uses subject names to denote message destinations, decoupling producers from consumers. Because of subject-based addressing, publish/subscribe is possible. Users can subscribe to the subjects that interest them, and information they need is automatically sent to them.

Subject name—The identifying name (and destination address) of any message (broadcast or point-to-point). *See* subject-based addressing.

Superfine market segmentation—Focusing product/service invention to meet the needs of individual customers, as opposed to generalized market segments.

T1 and T3 lines—Digital WAN carrier facility that transmits data at 1.544 Mbps through the telephone switching network and is the common connectivity method for most large corporations. T3 lines are even faster at 44.736 Mbps, enough for full-motion video.

TCP/IP (Transmission Control Protocol/Internet Protocol)—The communications protocols that underlie the Internet. Originally used and developed by the U.S. Department of Defense in the 1970s for the DARPA network. To be on the Internet, your computer must have TCP/IP software.

TIB (The Information Bus)—TIBCO's core technology for creating a real-time information distribution infrastructure.

TK—Yahoo!'s famous CEO Tim Koogle. To do a "TK" means to start an Internet company and to make it vastly successful.

TQM (Total Quality Management)—A management philosophy geared toward the continuous improvement of quality to meet, exceed, and anticipate customer expectations.

URL (Uniform Resource Locator)—The standard method for giving the address for resources on the World Wide Web.

User experience—The experience of users on a portal site. The better the user experience the more likely you can attract and keep eyeballs.

Virtual supply network—A term that refers to the electronic integration of the supply chain. Virtual means that information and services outside the enterprise (those of partners, suppliers, and customers) are integrated with internal content from the enterprise in a single, seamless flow of real-time information, possibly over the Internet.

VPN (Virtual Private Network)—A private data network, which uses the public telecommunication infrastructure, but maintains privacy through security procedures, encryption of data, and tunneling. Companies use VPNs for both extranets and wide area intranets.

Workstation—A PC or terminal connected to a network.

WWW—The World Wide Web, which is a the collection of resources that can be accessed using tools such as Gopher, FTP, HTTP, and Telnet, allowing files and information to be shared.

xDSL (Digital Subscriber Line)—Any of a range of DSL technologies that allow wideband communication over existing twisted-pair wiring. High-rate services can be offered using these technologies (ranging as high as 52 Mbps) more economically than other high bandwidth technologies requiring special cabling.

XML (Extensible Markup Language)—A way of representing data and metadata so that they may be easily shared among multiple applications and organizations.

Zero lag—Without delay. Event-driven.

Zero latency—A term coined by the Gartner Group that is similar to event-driven. In a zero-latency enterprise, as in an event-driven enterprise, there is no delay between when a business event occurs and when the relevant parts of the enterprise are apprised of the event and can respond. Implies real-time infrastructure capabilities.

REFERENCES

1. P. Drucker, *Managing in a Time of Great Change* (New York: Truman Talley/Dutton, 1995), 236.

2. T. A. Stewart, *Intellectual Capital: The New Wealth of Organizations* (New York: Doubleday, 1997), foreword.

3. M. E. Porter, *Competitive Strategies: Techniques for Analyzing Industries and Competitors* (New York: The Free Press, 1980), 6.

4. M. M. Waldrop, *Complexity: The Emerging Science at the Edge of Order and Chaos* (New York: Touchstone Books, 1993), 11–12.

5. A. de Geus, *The Living Company* (Boston, Harvard Business School Press, 1997), 21.

6. T. Peters, *Thriving on Chaos: Handbook for a Management Revolution* (New York: Knopf, 1987), 67.

7. R. McKenna, *Real Time: Preparing for the Age of the Never-Satisfied Customer* (Boston: Harvard Business School Press, 1997), 11.

8. ActiveMedia, "Future Scapes: Impacts of the 'Net on Core Economic Factors," www.activemedia.com, online publication.

9. U.S. Commerce Department, "Building Out the Internet," in *The Emerging Digital Economy* (April 1998).

10. Reuters, "Worldwide Internet Use to Reach 130.6 Million," *TechWeb* (July 7, 1999), online publication.

11. "E-Commerce Market Could Hit $3.2 Trillion by 2003," *Information Week* (November 6, 1998), online publication.

12. C. Meyer, *Relentless Growth: How Silicon Valley Strategies Can Work in Your Business* (New York: The Free Press, 1998), 48.

13. L. Donaldson and F. G. Hilmer, *Management Redeemed: Debunking the Fads That Undermine Corporate Performance* (New York: The Free Press, 1996).

14. D. K. Smith, *Taking Charge of Change: 10 Principles for Managing People and Performance* (New York: Addison-Wesley, 1996), 2.

15. R. E. Miles et al., "Organizing in the Knowledge Age: Anticipating the Cellular Form," *Academy of Management Executive* 11 (1997): 7–24.

16. L. C. Thurow, *The Future of Capitalism: How Today's Economic Forces Shape Tomorrow's World* (New York: William Morrow, 1996), 6.

17. P. Ormerod, *The Death of Economics* (New York: John Wiley & Sons, 1997), 173–176.

18. R. Stacey, *Managing the Unknowable: Strategic Boundaries Between Order & Chaos in Organizations* (San Francisco: Jossey-Bass, 1992), 124.

19. D. Hancock, interview with author, October 1996.

20. B. Arthur, "Increasing Returns and the New World of Business," *Harvard Business Review* (July/August 1996): 108–109.

21. D. Peppers and M. Rogers, *The One-to-One Future: Building Relationships One Customer at a Time* (New York: Doubleday, 1993), user's guide.

22. M. Hammer, *Beyond Reengineering: How the Process-Centered Organization Is Changing Our Work and Our Lives* (New York: HarperBusiness, 1996), 36.

23. McKenna, *Real Time*, 169.

24. Meyer, *Relentless Growth*, 29.

25. D. Peppers and M. Rogers, *Enterprise One-to-One: Tools for Competing in the Interactive Age* (New York: Doubleday, 1997), 16.

26. Ibid., 385.

27. B. Arthur, "Increasing Returns and the New World of Business," 108–109.

28. Peppers and Rogers, *Enterprise One-to-One*, 390–391.

29. Ibid.

30. C. Meyer, *Fast Cycle Time: How to Align Purpose, Strategy, and Structure for Speed* (New York: The Free Press, 1993), 48.

31. E. Wyatt, "Shares of Wealth in Stock Holdings Hit 50-Year High," *New York Times* (February 11, 1998).

32. J. Berst, "Get on Board the Multicast Bandwagon," ZD-*Net* (February 9, 1998), online publication.

33. J. Marshall, "Tolls Rising on Information Highway: Faster Net Access Has a Big Price," *San Francisco Chronicle* (February 12, 1998).

34. Stewart, *Intellectual Capital*, xx, foreword.

35. L. J. Flynn, "Push, the Hot New Technology of '97, Gets a Cold Shoulder in '98," *New York Times* (February 16, 1998).

36. Berst, "Get on Board."

37. C. O'Dell, as quoted in D. Stamps, "The Self-Organizing System," *Training* (April 1997): 8.

38. C. Meyer, *Fast Cycle Time*, 74.

39. McKenna, *Real Time*, 159.

40. C. Tristam, "Middleware Makes C/S Apps Really Work," *Datamation* 42 (August 1996): 78–83.

41. International Data Corporation: "Middleware Moves to Achieve Universal Acceptance," report (1996).

42. J. Gantz, A. Giraldo, C. Glasheen, and M. Sullivan-Trainor, "Internet Futures Spending Model, 1997–2002: Business Gears Up for E-Commerce," IDC report (January 1999): 14.

43. Marshall, "Tolls Rising on Information Highway."

44. P. Drucker, Fortune IT Strategy Forum, Pebble Beach, CA (*Information Week*, February 16, 1998).

45. L. Kaufman, *New York Times on the Web* (May 24, 1999), online publication.

46. "The E-Corporation," *Fortune Magazine* 138 (December 7, 1998).

47. "AOL Members Spent More Than $1B over the Holidays," *PCWeek Online* (January 4, 1999), Boston Consulting Group and shop.org study.

48. Miles et al., "Organizing in the Knowledge Age."

49. J. F. Moore, *The Death of Competition: Leadership and Strategy in the Age of Business Ecosystems* (New York: HarperCollins, 1996), 13.

50. C. Handy, *The Age of Unreason* (Boston: Harvard Business School Press, 1989), 5.

51. S. Caulken, "Chaos Inc.," *Across the Board*, 32 (July/August 1995): 34.

52. Waldrop, *Complexity*, 293.

53. Stewart, *Intellectual Capital*.

54. "Powerpack Man," *Fast Company* (August 1997), online publication.

55. W. M. Cohen and D. A. Levinthal, "Absorptive Capacity: A New Perspective on Learning and Innovation," *Administrative Science Quarterly* (March 1990), 9.

56. de Geus, *The Living Company*, 21.

57. S. Ross, "Companies That Value Learning Are Good Workplaces," *St. Louis Post-Dispatch* (December 1997).

58. M. Treacy and F. Wiersema, *The Discipline of Market Leaders: Choose Your Customers, Narrow Your Focus, Dominate Your Market* (New York: Addison-Wesley, 1997), xii–xiii.

59. S. E. Gross, *Compensation for Teams: How to Design and Implement Team-Based Reward Programs* (New York: American Management Association, 1995), 7–11.

60. de Geus, *The Living Company*, 21.

61. Stacey, *Managing the Unknowable*, 186.

62. J. P. Kotter, *Leading Change* (Boston: Harvard Business School Press, 1996), 125.

63. M. Brooks (director). *The Twelve Chairs*, 20th Century Fox, 1970.

64. Stacey, *Managing the Unknowable*, 124–125.

65. Hammer, *Beyond Reengineering*, 91.

66. Drucker, *Managing in a Time of Great Change*, 236.

67. Stewart, *Intellectual Capital*, 90–93.

68. Ibid., 101.

69. M. Walton, *The Deming Management Method* (New York: Perigree, 1998), 143.

70. Stewart, *Intellectual Capital*, 101.

71. G. Hamel and C. K. Prahalad, *Competing for the Future: Breakthrough Strategies for Seizing Control of Your Industry and Creating the Markets of Tomorrow* (Boston, MA: Harvard Business School Press, 1996), 290.

72. Handy, *The Age of Unreason*, 125.

73. P. Drucker, *The Drucker Foundation: The Leader of the Future* (San Francisco: Jossey-Bass, 1996), xii, foreword.

74. C. W. Pollard, "The Leader Who Serves," in *The Leader of the Future* (San Francisco: Jossey-Bass, 1996), 241.

75. Peters, *Thriving on Chaos,* 514.

76. Meyer, *Relentless Growth*, 41.

77. Hamel and Prahalad, *Competing for the Future*, 134.

78. Ibid., 133.

79. J. P. Kotter, *Leading Change* (Boston: Harvard Business School Press, 1996), 72, 77.

80. Ibid.

81. Smith, *Taking Charge of Change*.

82. Peppers and Rogers, *Enterprise One-to-One,* 16.

83. Hamel and Prahalad, *Competing for the Future*, 99–100.

84. Peppers and Rogers, *The One-to-One Future*, user's guide.

85. F. Reichheld, *The Loyalty Effect* (Boston, MA: Harvard Business School Press, 1996), 37.

86. Peppers and Rogers, *The One-to-One Future*, 173–206.

87. J. H. Gilmore and B. J. Pine II, "The Four Faces of Mass Customization," *Harvard Business Review* (January/February 1997), 91–101.

88. Ibid.

89. McKenna, *Real Time*, 86, 98, 109–110, 142, 152.

90. D. Peppers and M. Rogers, "Marketing One-to-One" (March 12, 1998), online newsletter.

91. Moore, *The Death of Competition*, 13.

92. Miles et al., "Organizing in the Knowledge Age."

93. "To Byte the Hand That Feeds: Firms and Their Suppliers," *The Economist* 346 (January 17, 1998): 61–62.

94. Smith, *Taking Charge of Change*, 2–3.

95. Peppers and Rogers, *Enterprise One-to-One,* 388.

96. D. A. Nadler and M. L. Tushman, "Beyond the Charismatic Leader: Leadership and Organizational Changes," *California Management Review*, 32 (Winter 1990): 81–83.

97. Peppers and Rogers, *Enterprise One-to-One*, 389.

98. Institute for the Future, "1998 Ten-Year Forecast: From Information to Knowledge—Harnessing the Talent of the Twenty-First Century Workforce" (1998): 165.

99. A. Carnevale and S. Rose, *Education for What? The New Office Economy* (Princeton, NJ: Educational Testing Service, 1998), 8–11.

100. Ibid.

101. J. Mardick, "Waiting for the Computer Revolution," *New York Review of Books* (March 26, 1998), online publication.

102. Ibid.

103. Ibid.

INDEX